spud and chloë
at the farm

Also by
Susan B. Anderson

Itty-Bitty Hats
Itty-Bitty Nursery
Itty-Bitty Toys

spud and chloë
at the farm

susan b. anderson

photographs by liz banfield

ARTISAN

new york

Published by Artisan
A Division of Workman Publishing Company, Inc.
225 Varick Street
New York, NY 10014-4381
www.artisanbooks.com

Published simultaneously in Canada by Thomas Allen & Son, Limited

Library of Congress Cataloging-in-Publication Data
Anderson, Susan B.
Spud and Chloë at the farm / Susan B. Anderson.
photographs by Liz Banfield
  p. cm.
ISBN 978-1-57965-430-6
1. Knitting—Patterns. 2. Soft toy making. 3. Farms—Juvenile fiction. I. Title.
TT825.A5554 2011
746.43'2—dc22   2010039572

Printed in China
First printing, March 2011

10 9 8 7 6 5 4 3 2 1

To my loving family

and

to Linda, for thinking up Spud and Chloë,
without whom none of this would be

Contents

Introduction

A couple of years ago, Blue Sky Alpacas, a popular yarn company, asked me to design some chubby chickens for them. I guess my name had come up at their staff meeting as the go-to chubby-chicken designer. I was honored to be approached by one of the most admired companies in the fiber industry. Of course I took the assignment and ran with it—which was kismet, since it grew into something more, something wonderful.

In the summer of 2009, Blue Sky Alpacas introduced a new product line called Spud & Chloë. I loved the samples they sent me, and I was pleased to do designing for this fresh line, with its innovative mod colors and product design. At the same time, Spud & Chloë conveyed a sweet innocence and a bit of a vintage feeling—it made me remember what it was like to be a child. "Sweet yarns for real life" is Spud & Chloë's philosophy, and it rings true to the core.

Then Blue Sky Alpacas asked me to be the curator of Spud says!, an adorable blog for the Spud & Chloe Web site. Through this work I've gotten to know the public faces of the line: Spud, an introverted but lovable sheep, and Chloë, his owner, who's more of an upbeat cheerleader type. These two lead characters became a part of the fabric of my daily life, and I realized a book would be the next natural progression of our adventures together. That's how the book version of Spud & Chloë was born. And what better setting could there be to start the adventures of Spud & Chloë than a farm? This environment gives me yet another chance to create and knit some adorable animals, cute characters for Spud and Chloë to meet. The adventures of Spud and Chloë have begun.

Spud & Chloë at the Farm departs from my earlier books, in that it doesn't include basic knitting techniques. All that information can be found in my online tutorials, on other online instructional knitting Web sites, and elsewhere. Meanwhile, I'm happy to incorporate a new element into this book.

Interestingly, this came about from something that happened when my last book, *Itty-Bitty Toys*, was published. I constantly heard from knitters that their children interacted just as much with the book as the knitters themselves. In fact, many knitters told me that their kids used *Itty-Bitty Toys* like a catalog, dog-earing the pages and placing their toy orders. It was great to know that my knitting projects were helping adults and children bond as they discussed the progress on a particular toy and so on, and incorporating a simple narrative that a knitter and child could share seemed like a natural next step. So *Spud & Chloë at the Farm* includes a little children's story about the title characters' visit woven throughout its pages. My hope is that while you enjoy the book as the knitter of the projects, the children around you can also enjoy the illustrated story, which is repeated in full at the back of the book. You might even want to read it aloud together!

Finally, I should mention that the yarn from this marvelous line is made from all-natural fibers. Two of the lines contain certified organic cotton. All of the yarns are also machine-washable, which is an enormous plus in my estimation!

So it's time to join the adorable Spud and Chloë on their visit to the farm. I hope you enjoy this knitting adventure!

Abbreviations

dpn(s)	double-pointed needle(s)
k	knit
k2tog	knit two stitches together
kfb	knit in the front and back of the same stitch
m1	make 1 stitch by placing the bar in between the stitches on the left needle and knitting through the back loop
mb	make bobble (see page 57)
p	purl
p2tog	purl two stitches together

pfb	purl in the front and back of the same stitch
rem	remain
rnd(s)	round(s)
sl	slip a stitch
ssk	slip two stitches one at a time as if to knit, and knit these two stitches together through the back loop
st(s)	stitch(es)
tl	twisted loop (see pages 26 and 79)

Off to the Farm

I begin this farm adventure by introducing the two main characters, Chloë and her sheep, Spud. Chloë starts the day with an invitation to the farm of their friend Little Lamb. You'll discover more about Spud and Chloë and their buddies as you knit and read the story on the pages ahead.

Come on! Let's get started!

Chloë

Meet Chloë. Her bright, shiny personality comes to life as you stitch her adorable blue jumper and red Mary Jane shoes, and create her gorgeous red ponytail. Chloë is the type to make lemonade out of lemons every chance she gets. Her positive outlook is bound to rub off on her sheep Spud at some point.

Finished Measurements
10 inches tall from the feet to the top of the head, 2½ inches wide across the body

Yarn
Spud & Chloë Sweater (55% superwash wool, 45% organic cotton; 100 grams/160 yards), 1 hank each in Toast #7506, Firecracker #7509, and Splash #7510

Needles
U.S. size 5 (3.75 mm) double-pointed needles (set of four) or size needed to obtain gauge
U.S. size 7 (4.5 mm) double-pointed needles (set of four) or size needed to obtain gauge

Notions
Stitch markers
Ruler or tape measure
Yarn needle
Scissors
Plastic pellets (optional—do not use for young children or babies, as they pose a choking hazard)
Polyester fiberfill
Embroidery needle
Brown, white, and red embroidery floss
Stitch holder

Gauge
6 sts per inch in stockinette stitch for the doll and Mary Janes
5 sts per inch in stockinette stitch for the dress

BODY

Starting at the bottom of the body and using the smaller needles, cast on 9 sts with Toast, placing 3 sts on each of three dpns. Join to work in the round, being careful not to twist the stitches. Place a stitch marker on the first stitch.

Rnd 1: Knit.

Rnd 2: Kfb in each st—6 sts per needle, 18 sts total.

Rnds 3 and 4: Knit.

Rnd 5: (k2, kfb); repeat to the end of the round—8 sts per needle, 24 sts total.

Rnd 6: Knit.

Rnd 7: (k3, kfb); repeat to the end of the round—10 sts per needle, 30 sts total.

Rnd 8: Knit.

Rnd 9: (k4, kfb); repeat to the end of the round—12 sts per needle, 36 sts total.

Place a stitch marker on round 9 and leave it there. Knit every round until the body measures 3¼ inches above the stitch marker.

Decrease Rounds

Rnd 1: (k4, k2tog); repeat to the end of the round—10 sts per needle, 30 sts rem.

Rnd 2: Knit.

Rnd 3: (k3, k2tog); repeat to the end of the round—8 sts per needle, 24 sts rem.

Rnd 4: (k2, k2tog); repeat to the end of the round—6 sts per needle, 18 sts rem.

After round 4, thread the tail from the cast-on sts on a yarn needle and take some stitches, pulling tight to close the hole. Pull the tail through to the inside and trim.

Fill the body one-quarter full with plastic pellets and stuff the rest with fiberfill *or* stuff only with fiberfill until the body is firm. Continue stuffing the body to the end of the Decrease rounds.

Rnd 5: (k1, k2tog); repeat to the end of the round—4 sts per needle, 12 sts rem.

Rnd 6: (k2, k2tog); repeat to the end of the round—3 sts per needle, 9 sts rem.

Complete stuffing the body. Cut the yarn, thread it on a yarn needle, and draw it through the remaining sts, pulling tight to close the hole. Pull the end through to the inside and trim.

HEAD

Starting at the bottom of the head and using the smaller needles, cast on 9 sts with Toast, placing 3 sts on each of three dpns. Join to work in the round, being careful not to twist the stitches. Place a stitch marker on the first stitch.

Rnd 1: Knit.

Rnd 2: Kfb in each st—6 sts per needle, 18 sts total.

Rnds 3 and 4: Knit.

Rnd 5: (k2, kfb); repeat to the end of the round—8 sts per needle, 24 sts total.

Rnd 6: Knit.

Rnd 7: (k3, kfb); repeat to the end of the round—10 sts per needle, 30 sts total.

Rnd 8: Knit.

Rnd 9: (k4, kfb); repeat to the end of the round—12 sts per needle, 36 sts total.

Rnds 10–23: Knit.

Decrease Rounds

Rnd 24: (k4, k2tog); repeat to the end of the round—10 sts per needle, 30 sts rem.

Rnd 25: (k3, k2tog); repeat to the end of the round—8 sts per needle, 24 sts rem.

Rnd 26: (k2, k2tog); repeat to the end of the round—6 sts per needle, 18 sts rem.

After round 26, thread the end from the cast-on sts on a yarn needle. Take some stitches, pulling tight to close the hole. Leave the end on the outside to use later.

Stuff the head with fiberfill until firm. Continue to stuff the head until the end of the Decrease rounds.

Rnd 27: (k1, k2tog); repeat to the end of the round—4 sts per needle, 12 sts rem.

Rnd 28: (k2, k2tog); repeat to the end of the round—3 sts per needle, 9 sts rem.

Complete stuffing the head. Cut the yarn, thread it on a yarn needle, and draw it through the remaining sts, pulling tight to close the hole. Pull the end through to the inside and trim.

Thread the end from the cast-on sts on a yarn needle and whipstitch the bottom of the head to the top of the body. Pull the end to the inside and trim.

I'll tell Spud about going to Little Lamb's farm today. Maybe I could get him to come with me.

ARMS (Make 2)

Starting at the top shoulder and using the smaller needles, cast on 3 sts with Toast. Use two dpns to work back and forth.

Row 1: Knit.

Row 2: Pfb, p1, pfb—5 sts.

Row 3: Knit.

Row 4: Pfb, p3, pfb—7 sts.

Row 5: Knit.

Row 6: Pfb, p5, pfb—9 sts.

Row 7: Knit.

Place 3 sts on each of three dpns. Join to work in the round, being careful not to twist the stitches. Place a stitch marker on the first stitch. Knit every round until the arm measures 2 inches from the joining round.

Wrist and Hand

Rnd 1: (k1, k2tog); repeat to the end of the round—2 sts per needle, 6 sts rem.

Rnd 2: Knit.

Rnd 3: (k1, m1, k1); repeat to the end of the round—3 sts per needle, 9 sts total.

Rnds 4–7: Knit.

Rnd 8: (k1, k2tog); repeat to end of round—2 sts per needle, 6 sts rem.

Cut the yarn, thread it on a yarn needle, and draw it through the remaining sts, pulling tight to close the hole. Fill the hand with plastic pellets and stuff the rest of the arm with fiberfill until firm *or* only stuff with fiberfill.

Thread the end from the cast-on sts on a yarn needle. Lay the arm flat from the cast-on edge to the joining round. Whipstitch the top of the arm closed. Whipstitch the arm to the side of the body. Pull the end to the inside and trim.

LEGS (Make 2)

Starting at the top of the leg and using the smaller needles, cast on 9 sts with Toast, placing 3 sts on each of three dpns. Join to work in the round, being careful not to twist the stitches. Place a stitch marker on the first stitch.

Knit every round until the leg measures 3¼ inches from the beginning.

Ankle and Foot

Rnd 1: (k1, k2tog); repeat to the end of the round—2 sts per needle, 6 sts rem.

Rnd 2: Knit.

Rnd 3: (k1, m1, k1); repeat to the end of the round—3 sts per needle, 9 sts total.

Rnds 4–8: Knit.

Rnd 9: (k1, k2tog); repeat to the end of the round—2 sts per needle, 6 sts rem.

Cut the yarn, thread it on a yarn needle, and draw it through the

remaining sts, pulling tight to close the hole. Secure the end and pull it through to the inside and back out again at the ankle. Leave the end there for now.

Fill the foot with plastic pellets and the rest of the leg with fiberfill until firm *or* use fiberfill only.

Using the yarn from the ankle that was left earlier, take a couple of stitches to attach the top of the foot to the ankle, making the foot bend forward. Secure the end, pull it through to the inside of the leg, and trim.

Thread the end from the cast-on sts on a yarn needle and whipstitch the leg to the bottom of the body. Secure the end, pull it through to the inside of the body, and trim.

EARS (Make 2)
Using the smaller needles, cast on 6 sts with Toast, placing 2 sts on each of three dpns. Join to work in the round, being careful not to twist the stitches.

Knit 1 round.

Cut the yarn, thread it on a yarn needle, and draw it through the stitches, pulling tight to close the hole. Stitch to secure, pull the end to the inside, and trim.

Thread the end from the cast-on sts on a yarn needle and whipstitch the ear to the side of the head. Pull the end to the inside of the head and trim.

I hope . . .

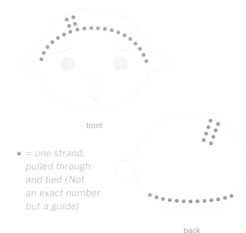

front

● = one strand,
pulled through
and tied (Not
an exact number
but a guide)

back

HAIR

With Firecracker, cut a few 12-inch strands at a time as you work, continuing to cut more strands until you have added enough. Thread 1 strand at a time on a yarn needle, pull each strand through a stitch on the head and along the hairline and part (see illustration for placement). Pull each strand through halfway and secure with a half-knot.

After completing hair placement along the entire hairline and two rows of hair strands for the side part, pull the hair into a ponytail. Secure it with another strand of Firecracker tied tightly in a full knot. Trim the ponytail to the desired length. Trim the strands so they aren't all the same length to give the hair a more textured appearance.

HAIR TIE

Cast on 5 sts with Splash, using the smaller needles. Use two dpns to work back and forth.

Row 1: Knit.
Row 2: Purl.
Row 3: Knit.
Row 4: Purl.
Row 5: K1, then k2tog twice—3 sts rem.

Begin to work in I-cord until the tie measures 4½ inches from the cast-on edge.

End of Tie
Row 1: Kfb, k1, kfb—5 sts.
Row 2: Purl.
Row 3: Knit.
Row 4: Purl.

Bind off. Cut the yarn and pull it through the remaining st. Use the yarn needle to weave in the ends to the purl side of the tie, and trim. Tie the hair tie around the ponytail and secure with a half-knot.

FACE

Note: Pull all ends to the inside and trim to stay inside of the head.

Eyes

With an embroidery needle and a length of brown embroidery floss, make 2 small spiderweb circles for the eyes (see illustration). With a length of white embroidery floss, take 2 tiny straight stitches to make flecks in the eyes.

Eyebrows

With an embroidery needle and a length of brown embroidery floss, take 2 small straight stitches above the eyes.

Mouth

With an embroidery needle and a length of red embroidery floss take 2 small straight stitches to form a V shape.

Nose

With a yarn needle and a length of Toast, take 2 straight stitches close together to form the nose.

Spiderweb circles for eyes

DRESS

With the larger dpns, cast on 48 sts with Splash, placing 16 sts on each of three dpns. Join to work in the round, being careful not to twist the stitches. Place a stitch marker on the first stitch.

Rnd 1: Knit.

Rnd 2: Purl.

Knit every round until the dress measures 3½ inches from the cast-on edge.

Bodice

Row 1: Bind off the first 3 sts, k20 sts onto one dpn (21 sts should be on the needle), turn. Place the other 24 sts on a stitch holder.

Row 2: Bind off the first 3 sts, purl to the end of the row—18 sts rem.

Row 3: K1, ssk, knit to the last 3 sts, k2tog, k1—16 sts rem.

Row 4: Purl.

Row 5: K1, ssk, knit to the last 3 sts, k2tog, k1—14 sts rem.

Row 6: Purl.

Row 7: K4, bind off 6 sts, k4, place the last 4 sts on a free dpn.

Straps

Now work in I-cord on the last 4 sts.

Row 1: K2tog twice—2 sts rem.

Continue working in I-cord until the strap measures 2½ inches from the start of the I-cord. Bind off. Cut the yarn and pull the end through the remaining st.

Now work the other 4 sts on the dpn the same as the first strap.

Back

Place the stitches from the stitch holder on a dpn. Reattach the yarn so you are ready to knit across the remaining 24 sts.

Row 1: (k1, k2tog); repeat to the end of the row—16 sts rem.

Bind off.

Thread the end on a yarn needle and whipstitch the straps to the bind-off edge of the back, measuring 2 inches from the sides of the front and with ¾ inch between the straps.

MARY JANES (Make 2)

Using the smaller needles, cast on 12 sts with Firecracker, placing 4 sts on each of three dpns.

Join to work in the round, being careful not to twist the stitches. Place a stitch marker on the first stitch.

Rnd 1: Knit.

Rnd 2: K2, k1 ([m1, k1] three times), k1 ([m1, k1] three times)—18 sts total remain.

Rnds 3 and 4: Knit.

Rnd 5: Purl.

Rnd 6: Knit.

Rnd 7: K2, k2tog twice, k3tog twice, k2tog twice, k2—10 sts rem.

Place 5 sts on each of two dpns. Use the Kitchener stitch to close the bottom of the shoe.

Straps (Make 2)

Using the smaller needles, cast on 2 sts with Firecracker. Use two dpns to work in I-cord until the strap measures 1½ inches from the cast-on edge. Bind off. Cut the yarn and pull through the remaining st.

Using the tails and a yarn needle, sew each end of the strap to the sides of the shoe.

Well, here goes. . . .

Spud

Spud is truly the star of the show, the center of attention, and the scene-stealer whether he likes it or not! I have used the wooly twisted loop stitch on Spud's body and hair to add depth and dimension to his coat. Spud is loads of fun to knit and even more fun to have around when completed.

Finished Measurements
8 inches tall (not including hair on head), 5 inches wide across the body, 5½ inches long from the front end of the body to the back end of the body

Yarn
Spud & Chloë Sweater (55% superwash wool, 45% organic cotton; 100 grams/160 yards), 1 hank each in Ice Cream #7500, Toast #7506, and Firecracker #7509

Needles
U.S. size 4 (3.5 mm) double-pointed needles (set of four) or size needed to obtain gauge

Notions
Stitch markers
Ruler or tape measure
Yarn needle
Scissors
Plastic pellets (optional—do not use for young children or babies, as they pose a choking hazard)
Polyester fiberfill
Embroidery needle
Black embroidery floss

Gauge
5½ sts per inch in stockinette stitch

Good morning, Spud.

I'm not much of a morning person—er, sheep.

Twisted Loop (tl)

Knit the stitch, leave it on the left needle, pull the loop from the right needle out 2 inches with your fingers. Place your finger in the loop and twist the loop until it folds over on itself. Place the loop on the left needle. Knit the 2 stitches together.

BODY

Starting at the base of the body, cast on 9 sts with Ice Cream, placing 3 sts on each of three dpns. Join to work in the round, being careful not to twist the stitches. Place a stitch marker on the first stitch.

Increase Rounds

Rnd 1 and every odd round: Knit.

Rnd 2: Kfb in each st—6 sts per needle, 18 sts total.

Rnd 4: (k1, kfb); repeat to the end of the round—9 sts per needle, 27 sts total.

Rnd 6: (k2, kfb); repeat to the end of the round—12 sts per needle, 36 sts total.

Rnd 8: (k3, kfb); repeat to the end of the round—15 sts per needle, 45 sts total.

Rnd 10: (k4, kfb); repeat to the end of the round—18 sts per needle, 54 sts total.

Rnd 12: (k5, kfb); repeat to the end of the round—21 sts per needle, 63 sts total.

Rnd 14: (k6, kfb); repeat to the end of the round—24 sts per needle, 72 sts total.

Place a stitch marker on round 14 and leave it there.

Twisted Loop Pattern

Begin pattern as follows:

Rnd 1: (tl, k1); repeat to the end of the round.

Rnd 2: Knit.

Rnd 3: (k1, tl); repeat to the end of the round.

Rnd 4: Knit.

Repeat rounds 1–4 until the body measures 3 inches above the marker on round 14, ending with round 1.

Decrease Rounds

Rnd 1: (k6, k2tog); repeat to the end of the round—21 sts per needle, 63 sts rem.

Rnd 2: (k1, tl); repeat to the last st, k1.

Rnd 3: (k5, k2tog); repeat to the end of the round—18 sts per needle, 54 sts rem.

Rnd 4: (tl, k1); repeat to the end of the round.

Rnd 5: (k4, k2tog); repeat to the end of the round—15 sts per needle, 45 sts rem.

After round 5, thread the tail from the cast-on sts on a yarn needle and take some stitches to close the hole on the bottom. Stitch to secure, pull the end to the inside of the body, and trim.

Fill one-third full with plastic pellets and stuff the rest with fiberfill *or* stuff only with fiberfill up to the needles. Continue to add stuffing as you finish the Decrease rounds.

Rnd 6: (k1, tl); repeat to the last st, k1.

Rnd 7: (k3, k2tog); repeat to the end of the round—12 sts per needle, 36 sts rem.

Rnd 8: (tl, k1); repeat to the end of the round.

Rnd 9: (k2, k2tog); repeat to the end of the round—9 sts per needle, 27 sts rem.

Rnd 10: (k1, tl); repeat to the last st, k1.

Rnd 11: (k1, k2tog); repeat to the end of the round—6 sts per needle, 18 sts rem.

Rnd 12: (tl, k1); repeat to the end of the round.

Rnd 13: K2tog to the end of the round—3 sts per needle, 9 sts rem.

Add any remaining stuffing needed.

Cut the yarn, leaving a 6-inch tail, and thread it on a yarn needle. Draw it through the remaining sts and stitch to secure. Pull it through to the inside and trim so the end stays inside.

HEAD

Starting at the back of the head with Toast, cast on 9 sts, placing 3 sts on each of three dpns. Join to work in the round, being careful not to twist the stitches. Place a stitch marker on the first stitch.

Good news! We are invited to visit Little Lamb's farm today.

Hmmm?

Rnd 1: Knit.

Rnd 2: (k1, m1, k1, m1, k1); repeat on each needle—5 sts per needle, 15 sts total.

Rnds 3 and 4: Knit.

Rnd 5: (k1, [k1, m1 four times]) repeat between (and) on each needle—9 sts per needle, 27 sts total.

Rnds 6 and 7: Knit.

Rnd 8: (k3, m1); repeat 3 times on each needle—12 sts per needle, 36 sts total.

Rnds 9–20: Knit.

Rnd 21: (ssk, k8, k2tog); repeat on each needle—10 sts per needle, 30 sts rem.

Rnd 22: Knit.

Rnd 23: (ssk, k6, k2tog); repeat on each needle—8 sts per needle, 24 sts rem.

Rnds 24 and 25: Knit.

Rnd 26: (ssk, k4, k2tog); repeat on each needle—6 sts per needle, 18 sts rem.

Rnd 27: Knit.

Rnd 28: (k4, k2tog); repeat on each needle—5 sts per needle, 15 sts rem.

After round 28, thread the tail from the cast-on sts on a yarn needle and take stitches to close the hole at the back of the head. Stitch to secure, then pull the end to the inside and trim. Fill the head with fiberfill until firm. Continue adding stuffing until the Decrease rounds are completed.

Rnd 29: (k3, k2tog); repeat on each needle—4 sts per needle, 12 sts rem.

Rnd 30: (k2, k2tog); repeat on each needle—3 sts per needle, 9 sts rem.

Add any final stuffing needed. Cut the yarn, thread it on a yarn needle, and draw it through the remaining sts, pulling tight to close the hole. Stitch to secure, then pull the tail to the inside and trim.

With a length of Toast threaded on a yarn needle, whipstitch the head to the top front of the body. Pull the ends to the inside of the head or body and trim.

FEET (Make 4)

Cast on 15 sts with Toast, placing 5 sts on each of three dpns. Join to work in the round, being careful not to twist the stitches. Place a stitch marker on the first stitch.

Rnds 1–6: Knit.

Rnd 7: (k3, k2tog); repeat on each needle—4 sts per needle, 12 sts rem.

Rnd 8: Knit.

Rnd 9: (k2, k2tog); repeat on each needle—3 sts per needle, 9 sts rem.

Stuff the foot with fiberfill until firm. Cut the yarn, thread it on a yarn needle, and draw it through the remaining sts, pulling tight to close the hole. Stitch to secure, then pull the tail to the inside and trim.

Thread the tail from the cast-on sts on a yarn needle and whipstitch the foot to the bottom of the body.

EARS (Make 2)

Cast on 6 sts with Toast, placing 2 sts on each of three dpns. Join to work in the round, being careful not to twist the stitches. Place a stitch marker on the first stitch.
Rnds 1–3: Knit.
Rnd 4: (k1, m1, k1); repeat on each needle—3 sts per needle, 9 sts total.

Rnds 5 and 6: Knit.
Rnd 7: (k1, k2tog); repeat on each needle—2 sts per needle, 6 sts rem.

Cut the yarn and thread the tail on a yarn needle. Draw the tail through the remaining sts, pulling tight to close the hole. Pull the tail to the inside and trim. Flatten out the ear.

Thread the end from the cast-on sts on a yarn needle and whipstitch the ears to the head, using the photo as a guide. Pull the end to the inside of the head and trim.

TAIL

Cast on 12 sts with Ice Cream, placing 4 sts on each of three dpns. Join to work in the round, being careful not to twist the stitches. Place a stitch marker on the first stitch.
Rnds 1–3: Knit.
Rnd 4: (k2, k2tog); repeat on each needle—3 sts per needle, 9 sts rem.
Rnd 5: (k1, k2tog); repeat on each needle—2 sts per needle, 6 sts rem.

You'll meet new friends.
It might be good for you.

There's that word *good* again.

Cut the yarn, thread it on a yarn needle, and draw it through the remaining sts, pulling tight to close the hole. Stitch to secure, then pull the end to the inside and trim. Flatten out the tail. Thread the end from the cast-on sts on a yarn needle and whipstitch the tail to the back end, toward the top of the body. Pull the end to the inside and trim.

HAIR

Cast on 6 sts with Ice Cream. Use two dpns to work back and forth.

Row 1: Tl in each st.
Row 2: Knit.
Rows 3 and 4: Repeat rows 1 and 2.
Row 5: Repeat row 1.

Bind off. Cut the yarn and draw it through the remaining st. Thread the tail on a yarn needle and arrange and whipstitch the hair between the ears on the top of the head. Pull the tail through to the inside and trim.

FACE

With an embroidery needle and a length of black embroidery floss, take 2 straight stitches to make each eye. Make a V for the nose and take 3 straight stitches to complete the mouth, using the photograph as a guide. Pull all ends to the inside and trim to stay inside of the head.

BOW TIE

Cast on 12 sts with Firecracker, placing 4 sts on each of three dpns. Join to work in the round, being careful not to twist the stitches. Place a stitch marker on the first stitch.

Knit every round until the bow tie measures 1¾ inches from the cast-on edge. Place 6 sts on each of two dpns and graft them using the Kitchener stitch. With the end from the cast-on sts threaded on a yarn needle, whipstitch the other end closed.

Center Loop

Cast on 4 sts with Firecracker. Using

two dpns, work in I-cord until the center loop measures 2¾ inches from the cast-on edge. Bind off. Cut the yarn, thread it on a yarn needle, and draw it through the remaining st. Place the I-cord around the middle of the bow tie. Whipstitch the ends together to form a ring.

COLLAR

Cast on 2 sts with Firecracker. Using two dpns, work in I-cord until the collar measures 7½ inches from the cast-on sts. Continue on to make a bobble, working back and forth as follows:

Row 1: Kfb, kfb—4 sts.

Row 2: Purl.

Row 3: Knit.

Row 4: Purl.

Row 5: Knit, do not turn, pass the second, third, and fourth sts over and off the needle—1 st rem.

Cut the yarn, thread it on a yarn needle, and draw it through the remaining st. Gather up the bobble with a few stitches. Pull the end to the inside and trim.

Thread the tail from the cast-on sts on a yarn needle.

Stitch the cast-on end to the cord to form a loop that measures ¾ inch (big enough for the bobble to pass through but not too loose). Pull the collar through the back of the center loop on the bow tie. Place the collar around Spud's neck and pull the bobble through the loop.

LEASH

Cast on 2 sts with Firecracker. Using two dpns, work in I-cord until the leash measures 8 inches from the cast-on edge. Bind off. Cut the yarn, thread it on a yarn needle, and draw it through the remaining st. Stitch the bind-off end to the cord to form a ¾-inch loop. This loop will go on Spud's collar. On the other end of the I-cord make a loop the same way measuring 1 inch. Slip this loop over Chloë's hand.

Oh, Spud, you never know— you might even have fun!

I'll go, but I doubt the grass will be any tastier at Little Lamb's.

Meet the
Farm Friends

Now it's time to meet Spud and Chloë's farm friends. Exploring the farm in search of Little Lamb, they meet a diverse bunch of farm animals: a welcoming farm dog, a sweet brown cow, two playful piglets, a mother hen and her chicks, a striped barn cat, a few tiny mice, and finally a little lamb! After getting to know these farm characters, it will be difficult to resist casting on for each of them.

Farm Dog

Farms always have a dog or two running around keeping things in order. Farm Dog is the spirited greeter living at this farm. He is a barker and a jumper, but in the friendliest of ways. Have fun creating this silly dog with a big presence.

Finished Measurements
8 inches tall, 3 inches wide,
2½ inches long from the front
to the back end of the body

Yarn
Spud & Chloë Sweater (55%
superwash wool, 45% organic cotton;
100 grams/160 yards), 1 hank each
in Toast #7506, Root Beer #7503,
Ice Cream #7500, and Splash #7510

Needles
U.S. size 6 (4 mm) double-pointed
needles (set of four) or size needed to
obtain gauge

Notions
Stitch markers
Ruler or tape measure
Yarn needle
Scissors
Plastic pellets (optional—do not use
for young children or babies, as they
pose a choking hazard)
Polyester fiberfill
Embroidery needle
Black embroidery floss
Plastic drinking straw

Gauge
5½ sts per inch in stockinette stitch

BODY

Starting at the back end of the body, cast on 9 sts with Toast, placing 3 sts on each of three dpns. Join to work in the round, being careful not to twist the stitches. Place a stitch marker on the first stitch.

Rnd 1: Knit.

Rnd 2: Kfb in each st—6 sts per needle, 18 sts total.

Rnd 3: Knit.

Rnd 4: Kfb in each st—12 sts per needle, 36 sts total.

Rnds 5 and 6: Knit.

Rnd 7: (k3, kfb); repeat to the end of the round—15 sts per needle, 45 sts total.

Place a stitch marker at the beginning of round 8 and leave it there. Knit until the body measures 3 inches above the stitch marker.

Decrease Rounds

Rnd 1: (k3, k2tog); repeat to the end of the round—12 sts per needle, 36 sts rem.

Rnd 2: Knit.

Rnd 3: (k2, k2tog); repeat to the end of the round—9 sts per needle, 27 sts rem.

At this point, thread the tail from the cast-on sts on a yarn needle. Take a few stitches to close the hole. Pull the end to the inside of the body and trim. Fill the bottom with a layer of plastic pellets and stuff the rest of the body until firm with fiberfill *or* stuff with fiberfill only. Continue to stuff the body.

Rnd 4: Knit.

Rnd 5: (k1, k2tog); repeat to the end of the round—6 sts per needle, 18 sts rem.

Rnd 6: Knit.

Rnd 7: (k2tog); repeat to the end of the round—3 sts per needle, 9 sts rem.

Finish any stuffing. Cut the yarn, thread it on a yarn needle, and draw it through the remaining sts, pulling tight to close the hole. Stitch to secure. Leave the end out to use later for attaching the head.

HEAD

Starting at the back of the head, work rounds 1–8 the same as for the body—15 sts per needle, 45 sts total. Place a stitch marker on round 8 and leave it there. Knit every round until the head measures 1¼ inches above the stitch marker.

Decrease Rounds

Rnd 1: On Needle 1, knit. On Needles 2 and 3 (k3, k2tog), repeat to the end of the round—12 sts rem on Needles 2 and 3 needle; 39 sts rem.

Rnd 2: On Needle 1, knit. On Needles 2 and 3, (k2, k2tog), repeat to the end of the round—9 sts rem on Needles 2 and 3; 33 sts rem.

Rnd 3: Knit.

Rnd 4: On Needle 1, k1, ssk, k9, k2tog, k1—13 sts rem. On Needles 2 and 3, (k1, k2tog), repeat to the end of the round—6 sts rem on each needle; 25 sts rem.

Rnds 5–10: Knit.

Rnd 11: On Needle 1, k1, (k1, k2tog) four times—9 sts rem. On Needles 2 and 3, knit—21 sts rem.

Rnd 12: On Needle 1, (k1, k2tog) three times—6 sts rem. On Needles 2 and 3, knit—18 sts rem.

At this point, thread the tail from the cast-on sts on a yarn needle. Take a few stitches to close the hole, pull the tail to the inside of the head, and trim. Fill the head with fiberfill until firm. Continue to stuff the head as needed as you work.

Rnd 13: (k1, k2tog); repeat to the end of the round—4 sts per needle, 12 sts rem.

Rnd 14: Knit.

Rnd 15: (k1, k2tog, k1); repeat to the end of the round—3 sts per needle, 9 sts rem.

Finish any stuffing. Cut the yarn, thread it on a yarn needle, and draw it through the remaining sts, pulling tight to close the hole. Take a couple of stitches to secure, pull the end to the inside, and trim.

Thread the end from the top of the body on a yarn needle and whipstitch the head to the body.

EARS (Make 2)

Outer Ear

Cast on 7 sts with Root Beer. Use two dpns to work back and forth.

Row 1: Knit.

Row 2: Purl.

Rows 3–6: Repeat rows 1 and 2.

Row 7: Ssk, k3, k2tog—5 sts rem.

Row 8: Purl.

Row 9: Ssk, k1, k2tog—3 sts rem.

Row 10: Purl.

Row 11: Slip 1 st, k2tog, pass the slipped st over and off the left needle—1 st rem.

Cut the yarn and pull the end through the remaining st.

Inner Ear

Cast on 5 sts with Ice Cream. Use two dpns to work back and forth.

Looks like we have a greeter here.

Oh, Spud, that's just Farm Dog saying hello.

Rows 1–6: Same as for the outer ear.
Row 7: Ssk, k1, k2tog—3 sts rem.
Row 8: Purl.
Row 9: Slip 1, k2tog, pass the slipped st over and off the left needle—1 st rem.

Cut the yarn and pull the end through the remaining st.

Place the inner ear on the outer ear with the purl sides together. Thread an end from the inner ear on a yarn needle and whipstitch the inner and outer ears together around the edge. Thread an end from the outer ear on a yarn needle and whipstitch the ear to the top of the head. Pull the ends from the outer ear into the head and trim. Pull the ends from the inner ear between the layers and trim. Repeat with the other ear.

NOSE

Cast on 1 st with Root Beer. Use two dpns to work back and forth.
Row 1: Knit in the front and back and front again—3 sts.
Row 2: Purl.
Row 3: Knit, do not turn, pass the second and third sts over the first st and off the needle—1 st rem.

Cut the yarn and pull the end through the remaining st. Place the end on a yarn needle and whipstitch the nose to the front of the face. Pull all ends to the inside of the head and trim.

FACE

Note: Pull all ends to the inside and trim to stay inside of the head.

Eyes

With a length of black embroidery floss on an embroidery needle take 2 tiny straight horizontal stitches per eye and then take 1 vertical stitch slightly above the horizontal stitches to catch the stitches and pull them up. Repeat for the other eye.

Mouth

With a length of black embroidery floss threaded on an embroidery needle, take straight stitches to make a vertical line coming down from the center of the nose. Then take 2 straight stitches on each side of the vertical stitch to form the upturned mouth.

Looks like he needs the leash more than me.

BIB

Cast on 6 sts with Ice Cream. Use two dpns to work back and forth.

Row 1: K1, m1, k4, m1, k1—8 sts.
Row 2: Purl.
Row 3: K1, m1, k6, m1, k1—10 sts.
Row 4: Purl.
Row 5: Knit.
Row 6: Purl.
Rows 7–10: Repeat rows 5 and 6.
Row 11: K1, ssk, k4, k2tog, k1—8 sts rem.
Row 12: Purl.

Bind off. Cut the yarn, leaving an 8-inch end, and thread it on a yarn needle. Whipstitch the bib to the front of the body below the head. Pull the ends to the inside and trim.

LEGS (Make 4)

Cast on 9 sts with Toast, placing 3 sts on each of three dpns. Join to work in the round, being careful not to twist the stitches. Place a stitch marker on the first stitch.

Rnds 1–7: Knit.

Bind off. Cut the yarn and pull the end through the remaining st.

Paws (Make 4)

Starting at the back of the paw, cast on 12 sts with Root Beer, placing 4 sts on each of three dpns. Join to work in the round, being careful not to twist the stitches. Place a stitch marker on the first stitch.

Rnds 1–3: Knit.
Rnd 4: (k1, m1, k2, m1, k1); repeat on each needle—6 sts per needle, 18 sts total.
Rnds 5 and 6: Knit.
Rnd 7: (ssk, k2, k2tog); repeat on each needle—4 sts per needle, 12 sts total.

Place the first 6 sts on the first needle. Place the last 6 sts on a second needle. Cut the yarn and thread it on a yarn needle. Use the Kitchener stitch to close the end of the paw. Pull the end to the inside and trim. Stuff the paw lightly with fiberfill. Thread the end from the cast-on sts on a yarn needle and take stitches to close the hole at the back of the paw. Pull the end to the inside and trim.

Thread the end from the leg's cast-on sts on a yarn needle and whipstitch the leg to the top of the paw. Pull the end to the inside and trim. Place a 1-inch piece of drinking straw inside the leg. Place a small amount of fiberfill around the straw inside of the leg. Thread the end from the leg's bind-off sts on a yarn needle and whipstitch the leg to the underside of the body. Pull all ends to the inside of the body and trim.

TAIL

Cast on 9 sts with Root Beer, placing 3 sts on each of three dpns. Join to work in the round, being careful not to twist the stitches. Place a stitch marker on the first stitch.

Knit every round until the tail measures 1 inch from the cast-on edge.

Next rnd: K1, then k2tog to the end of the round—5 sts rem.

Next rnd: Knit.

Cut the yarn, thread it on a yarn needle, and draw it through the remaining sts, pulling tight to close the hole. Take a couple of stitches to secure, pull the end to the inside, and trim.

Stuff the tail lightly with fiberfill. Thread the end from the cast-on sts on a yarn needle and whipstitch the tail to the lower center back.

COLLAR

Cast on 3 sts with Splash. Use two dpns to work in I-cord for about 7 inches. Measure by trying the collar on the dog as you work to get the correct length. It should fit around the neck and be long enough to form a loop at the end. To make the bobble at the other end, work back and forth as follows:

Row 1: Kfb, k1, kfb—5 sts.

Row 2: Purl.

Row 3: Knit, do not turn. Pass the second, third, fourth, and fifth sts over the first st and off the needle— 1 st rem.

Cut the yarn, thread it on a yarn needle, and draw it through the remaining st. Take stitches to form the bobble into a ball shape, then pull the end to the inside and trim.

Thread the tail from the cast-on sts on a yarn needle and stitch down the other end of the collar to form a loop that the bobble can pass through snugly.

We are looking for Little Lamb. Can you help us?

Bark!

Wow. Impressive vocabulary.

Brown Cow

Every farm needs a big brown cow! This big but babyish cow makes the perfect companion for Spud's adventure. If you're a novice as far as knitting toys goes, this straightforward project is the perfect place to begin.

Finished Measurements
8 inches tall, 4½ inches wide, 5 inches long from the front to the back of the body

Yarn
Spud & Chloë Sweater (55% superwash wool, 45% organic cotton; 100 grams/160 yards), 1 hank each in Ice Cream #7500, Root Beer #7503, and Watermelon #7512

Needles
U.S. size 6 (4 mm) double-pointed needles (set of four) or size needed to obtain gauge
U.S. size 6 (4 mm) 16-inch circular needle (optional)

Notions
Stitch markers
Ruler or tape measure
Yarn needle
Scissors
Plastic pellets (optional—do not use for young children or babies, as they pose a choking hazard)
Polyester fiberfill

Gauge
5½ sts per inch in stockinette stitch

Hey, there's Brown Cow!

I thought *hay* was for horses.

BODY

Underside of Body

Starting at the underside of the body, cast on 5 sts with Ice Cream. Use two dpns to work back and forth.

Row 1: K1, m1, knit to the last st, m1, k1.

Row 2: Purl.

Repeat rows 1 and 2 until there are 19 sts. Work in stockinette stitch until the underside measures 3 inches from the cast-on edge, ending with a purl row.

Decrease Rows

Row 1: K1, ssk, knit to the last 3 sts, k2tog, k1.

Row 2: Purl.

Repeat rows 1 and 2 until 5 sts rem, ending with a row 2.

Next row: K1, ssk, k2tog—3 sts rem.

Next row: Purl.

Next row: K1, k2tog, pass the first st over the second st and off the needle—1 st rem.

Top of Body

Switch to Root Beer, and continue picking up stitches around the edge of the underside of the body. On Needle 1 (same needle that is holding the 1 st), pick up 20 sts. On Needle 2, pick up 20 sts. On Needle 3, pick up 19 sts, and transfer the first st in Ice Cream from Needle 1 to Needle 3 —60 sts total. Place a stitch marker

on the first stitch on the first needle. Continue working in the round.

Rnd 1: Knit.

Rnd 2: K1, (k3, m1) six times, k1; repeat on each needle—26 sts per needle, 78 sts total.

Place a stitch marker on Round 2 and leave it there. At this point, you can work onto a 16-inch circular needle or continue on the dpns. Knit every round until the body measures 3 inches above the marker.

Decrease Rounds

If you switched to a circular needle, work back onto the dpns, distributing 26 sts per needle.

Rnd 1: (k11, k2tog); repeat to the end of the round—24 sts per needle, 72 sts rem.

Rnd 2: (k10, k2tog); repeat to the end of the round—22 sts per needle, 66 sts rem.

Rnds 3 and 4: Knit.

Rnd 5: (k9, k2tog); repeat to the end of the round—20 sts per needle, 60 sts rem.

Rnd 6: (k8, k2tog); repeat to the end of the round—18 sts per needle, 54 sts rem.

Rnd 7: (k7, k2tog); repeat to the end of the round—16 sts per needle, 48 sts rem.

Rnd 8: Knit.

Rnd 9: (k6, k2tog); repeat to the end of the round—14 sts per needle, 42 sts rem.

At this point, fill the bottom of the body with a layer of plastic pellets and stuff the rest with fiberfill *or* stuff only with fiberfill. Continue to stuff the body with fiberfill until the end.

Rnd 10: (k5, k2tog); repeat to the end of the round—12 sts per needle, 36 sts rem.

Rnd 11: (k4, k2tog); repeat to the end of the round—10 sts per needle, 30 sts rem.

Rnd 12: (k3, k2tog); repeat to the end of the round—8 sts per needle, 24 sts rem.

Rnd 13: Knit.

Rnd 14: (k2, k2tog); repeat to the end of the round—6 sts per needle, 18 sts rem.

Rnd 15: (k2tog); repeat to the end of the round—3 sts per needle, 9 sts rem.

Finish any remaining stuffing. Cut the yarn, thread it on a yarn needle, and draw it through the remaining sts, pulling tight to close the hole. Take a few stitches to secure, pull the end to the inside of the body, and trim.

HEAD

Starting at the back of the head with Ice Cream, cast on 9 sts, placing 3 sts on each of three dpns. Join to work in the round, being careful not to twist the stitches. Place a stitch marker on the first stitch.

Can you help us find Little Lamb?

I'll tell you if I can wear the bow tie.

Rnd 1: Knit.

Rnd 2: Kfb in each st—6 sts per needle, 18 sts total.

Rnds 3 and 4: Knit.

Rnd 5: Kfb in each st—12 sts per needle, 36 sts total.

Rnds 6 and 7: Knit.

Rnd 8: (k2, kfb); repeat to the end of the round—16 sts per needle, 48 sts total.

Place a stitch marker on round 8 and leave it there. Knit every round until the head measures 2 inches above the stitch marker.

Decrease Rounds

Rnd 1: On Needle 1, ssk, knit to the last 2 stitches, k2tog—14 sts rem. On Needles 2 and 3, (k2, k2tog); repeat to the end of the round—12 sts per needle; 38 sts rem.

Rnd 2: Knit.

Rnd 3: On Needle 1, ssk, knit to the last 2 stitches, k2tog—12 sts rem. On Needles 2 and 3, (k1, k2tog); repeat to the end of the round—8 sts per needle; 28 sts rem.

Rnds 4–10: Knit.

At this point, thread the end from the cast-on sts on a yarn needle and take some stitches to close the hole, pulling up tight. Pull the end to the inside of the head and trim. Stuff the head with fiberfill, and continue to add stuffing through the final rounds.

Rnd 11: (k2, k2tog); repeat to the end of the round—21 sts rem.

Rnd 12: Knit.

Rnd 13: On Needle 1, (k1, k2tog) 3 times—6 sts rem. On Needles 2 and 3, knit—18 sts rem.

Rnd 14: (k1, k2tog) repeat to the end of the round—4 sts per needle, 12 sts rem.

Finish any final stuffing. Then place the first 6 sts on one dpn and the last 6 sts on a second dpn. Cut the yarn, leaving a 6-inch tail, and thread the tail on a yarn needle. Use the Kitchener stitch to graft the tip of the nose together. Pull the end to the inside of the head and trim.

With a length of Ice Cream threaded on a yarn needle, whipstitch the head to the front top of the body. The face should point in the same direction as the point on the underside. Pull the end to the inside of the head or body and trim.

EARS (Make 2)

Outer Ear

Cast on 7 sts with Root Beer. Using two dpns, work back and forth in stockinette stitch until the outer ear measures 1½ inches from the cast-on edge, ending with a purl row.

Next row: Ssk, k3, k2tog—5 sts rem.

Next row: P2tog, p1, p2tog—3 sts rem.

Bind off. Cut the yarn and pull the end through the remaining st.

Inner Ear

Cast on 5 sts with Watermelon. Using two dpns, work back and forth in stockinette stitch until the inner ear measures 1¼ inches from the cast-on edge, ending with a purl row.

Next row: Ssk, k1, k2tog—3 sts rem.

Next row: Purl.

Bind off. Pull the end through the remaining st.

Place the inner ear on the outer ear with the purl sides together. Thread an end from the inner ear on a yarn needle and whipstitch the outer and inner ears together. Pull the end between the layers and trim.

Thread the cast-on end of the outer ear on a yarn needle and whipstitch the cast-on sides of the outer ear together, starting at the bottom and taking up a couple of stitches from the cast-on edge. Whipstitch the ear to the side of the head, using the photo on page 44 as a guide.

LEGS (Make 4)

Cast on 15 sts with Root Beer, placing 5 sts on each of three dpns.

Join to work in the round, being careful not to twist the stitches. Place a stitch marker on the first stitch.

Rnds 1–9: Knit.

Switch to Ice Cream.

Rnds 10–15: Knit.

Rnd 16: (k3, k2tog); repeat on each needle—4 sts per needle, 12 sts rem.

Rnd 17: (k2, k2tog); repeat on each needle—3 sts per needle, 9 sts rem.

Spud?

Ummm, not a chance.

Cut the yarn, thread it on a yarn needle, and draw it through the remaining sts, pulling tight to close the hole. Pull the end to the inside, weave in, and trim.

Fill the leg about one-third full with plastic pellets and stuff the rest with fiberfill *or* stuff only with fiberfill. Thread the end from the cast-on sts on a yarn needle and whipstitch the leg to the underside of the body. Pull the end to the inside of the leg or body and trim.

TAIL

Cast on 4 sts with Root Beer. Use two dpns to work in I-cord until the tail measures 1 inch from the cast-on edge.

Next row: K2tog twice—2 sts rem.
Next row: K2tog—1 st rem.

Cut the yarn and pull the end through the remaining st.

With Ice Cream, make a 1-inch tassel with 8 wraps. Use the ends to attach the tassel to the pointy end of the tail. Thread the end from the cast-on sts on a yarn needle and whipstitch the tail to the back end of the body. Pull all ends to the inside of the body and trim.

FACE

Eyes

With a length of Root Beer threaded on a yarn needle, take 3 small split stitches for the eyelid. For the eyelashes, take 3 tiny straight stitches.

Nostrils

With a length of Root Beer threaded on a yarn needle, take 2 small straight stitches for each nostril.

Maybe later Brown Cow.
Spud, be nice.

I'm trying.

Piglets

These pesky Piglets are knit up in Spud & Chloë Fine. Because of the lightweight yarn and smaller needles, toy knitting in a sock-weight yarn always makes for a good project—and one that's simple, too! From their cute pink ears to their curly tails, this dynamic piglet duo is adorable. And with just one skein of sock yarn, you can make two piglets and even have yarn left over.

Finished Measurements
4½ inches tall, 2½ inches wide, 3 inches from front end to back end

Yarn
Spud & Chloë Fine (80% superwash wool, 20% silk; 65 grams/248 yards), 1 hank each in Tutu #7807 and Sassafras #7808

Needles
U.S. size 2 (2.75 mm) double-pointed needles (set of four) or size needed to obtain gauge

Notions
Stitch markers
Ruler or tape measure
Yarn needle
Scissors
Plastic pellets (optional—do not use for young children or babies, as they pose a choking hazard)
Polyester fiberfill
Embroidery needle
Black embroidery floss

Gauge
7½ sts per inch in stockinette stitch

Good morning, Piglets.

Good morning, and how do you do?

BODY

Starting at the back end of the body with Tutu, cast on 9 sts, placing 3 sts on each of three dpns. Join to work in the round, being careful not to twist the stitches. Place a stitch marker on the first stitch.

Rnd 1: Knit.

Rnd 2: Kfb in each st—6 sts per needle, 18 sts total.

Rnd 3: Knit.

Rnd 4: Kfb in each st—12 sts per needle, 36 sts total.

Rnds 5 and 6: Knit.

Rnd 7: (k3, kfb); repeat to the end of the round—15 sts per needle, 45 sts total.

Rnd 8: Knit.

Rnd 9: (k4, kfb); repeat to the end of the round—18 sts per needle, 54 sts total.

Place a stitch marker on round 9 and leave it there. Knit every round until the body measures 2½ inches above the stitch marker.

Thread the end from the cast-on sts on a yarn needle and take some stitches to close the hole on the back end of the body. Take a few stitches to secure, pull the end to the inside of the body, and trim. Fill the underside of the body with plastic pellets and stuff the rest of the body with fiberfill

or stuff with fiberfill only. Continue to add stuffing as needed.

Decrease Rounds

Rnd 1: (k7, k2tog); repeat to the end of the round—16 sts per needle, 48 sts rem.

Rnd 2: (k6, k2tog); repeat to the end of the round—14 sts per needle, 42 sts rem.

Rnds 3 and 4: Knit.

Rnd 5: (k5, k2tog); repeat to the end of the round—12 sts per needle, 36 sts rem.

Rnd 6: (k4, k2tog); repeat to the end of the round—10 sts per needle, 30 sts rem.

Rnd 7: Knit.

Rnd 8: (k3, k2tog); repeat to the end of the round—8 sts per needle, 24 sts rem.

Rnd 9: (k2, k2tog); repeat to the end of the round—6 sts per needle, 18 sts rem.

Rnd 10: K2tog, repeat to the end of the round—3 sts per needle, 9 sts rem.

Finish adding any stuffing and make sure the body is filled until firm. Cut the yarn, thread it on a yarn needle, and draw it through the remaining sts, pulling tight to close the hole. Stitch to secure, pull the end through to the inside of the body, and trim.

HEAD

Starting at the back of the head with Tutu, cast on 9 sts, placing 3 sts on each of three dpns. Join to work in the round, being careful not to twist the stitches. Place a stitch marker on the first stitch.

Work rounds 1–7 the same as for the start of the body—45 sts.

Place a stitch marker on round 7 and knit every round until the head measures 1 inch above the stitch marker.

Decrease Rounds

Rnd 1: (k3, k2tog); repeat to the end of the round—12 sts per needle, 36 sts rem.

Rnd 2: (k2, k2tog); repeat to the end of the round—9 sts per needle, 27 sts rem.

Rnd 3: Knit.

Rnd 4: (k1, k2tog); repeat to the end of the round—6 sts per needle, 18 sts rem.

Rnd 5: Knit.

At this point, thread the tail from the cast-on sts on a yarn needle and take some stitches to close the hole at the back end of the head. Take a few stitches to secure, pull the tail to the inside of the head, and trim. Stuff the head until firm. Continue to add stuffing as needed while you finish the head and snout.

Rnds 6–11: Knit.

Rnd 12: (k1, k2tog); repeat to the end of the round—4 sts per needle, 12 sts rem.

Rnd 13: (k1, k2tog, k1); repeat on each needle—3 sts per needle, 9 sts rem.

Hey! Watch the wool with the muddy pig feet!

No worries, Spud, you're wash and wear, remember?

Cut the yarn, thread it on a yarn needle, and draw it through the remaining sts, pulling tight to close the hole. Take a couple of stitches to secure, pull the end to the inside of the head, and trim.

Thread a length of Tutu on a yarn needle and whipstitch the head to the top front of the body. Stitch to secure, pull the end to the inside of the head or body, and trim.

EARS (Make 2)

Cast on 9 sts with Sassafras, placing 3 sts on each of three dpns. Join to work in the round, being careful not to twist the stitches. Place a marker on the first stitch.

Rnds 1–4: Knit.
Rnd 5: (k1, k2tog) on each needle—2 sts per needle, 6 sts rem.
Rnd 6: K2tog; repeat to the end of the round—3 sts rem.

Place the 3 sts on one needle, k3tog—1 st rem.

Cut the yarn, thread it on a yarn needle, and draw it through the remaining st, pulling tight. Pull the tail through to the inside of the ear and trim.

Lay the ear flat and whipstitch the cast-on edge closed. Whipstitch the ears to the top of the head. Pull the ends to the inside of the head and trim.

NOSE

Cast on 3 sts with Sassafras. Use two dpns to work back and forth.
Row 1: Kfb, k1, kfb—5 sts.
Row 2: Purl.
Row 3: Knit.
Row 4: Purl.
Row 5: Ssk, k1, k2tog—3 sts rem.

Bind off in purl. Cut the yarn and draw the end through the last st. Thread the tail on a yarn needle and whipstitch the nose to the tip of the snout. Pull the end through to the inside of the snout and trim.

LEGS (Make 4)

Cast on 12 sts with Tutu, placing 4 sts on each of three dpns. Join to work in the round, being careful not to twist the stitches. Place a stitch marker on the first stitch.

Knit every row until the leg measures 1 inch from the cast-on edge.

Next row: K2tog; repeat to the end of the round—6 sts rem.

Cut the yarn, thread it on a yarn needle, and draw it through the remaining sts, pulling tight to close the hole. Take several stitches to secure, pull the end to the inside of the leg, and trim.

Fill the leg about one-third full with plastic pellets and stuff the rest

with fiberfill until firm *or* stuff with fiberfill only. When all four legs are completed, position the legs and whipstitch them to the underside of the body using the end from each leg's cast-on sts and a yarn needle.

TAIL
Cast on 10 sts with Tutu. Using two dpns, bind off tightly. Cut the yarn, thread it on a yarn needle, and draw it through the last st. Then whipstitch

the tail to the back end of the body. Pull both ends to the inside of the body and trim.

FACE
With an embroidery needle and black embroidery floss, make two eyes with tiny straight stitches. Make two nostrils using straight stitches on the tip of the snout. Pull all ends to the inside of the head and trim.

Are you here for the party?

Party? Are you trying to pull the wool over my eyes?

Look, there's Mother Hen.

Mother Hen
and Chicks

Mothers like to keep their little ones close, and Mother Hen is no exception to that rule. When you lift Mother Hen up, her hatching chicks are waiting underneath. The chicks can be removed from their shells. This interactive set is sure to please all of the chicken lovers out there.

Finished Measurements
Mother Hen: 6 inches tall including the crown, 4 inches wide
Chicks: 2¾ inches tall, 1¼ inches wide

Yarn
Spud & Chloë Sweater (55% superwash wool, 45% organic cotton; 100 grams/160 yards), 1 hank each in Ice Cream #7500, Firefly #7505, Pollen #7508, and Firecracker #7509

Needles
U.S. size 6 (4 mm) double-pointed needles (set of four) or size needed to obtain gauge

Notions
Stitch markers
Ruler or tape measure
Yarn needle
Scissors

Polyester fiberfill (small amount)
Plastic pellets (optional—do not use for young children or babies, as they pose a choking hazard)
Embroidery needle
Black embroidery floss

Gauge
5½ sts per inch in stockinette stitch

Make Bobble (mb)
Knit in the front and back and in the front again (3 sts) of the same st, turn, purl 3, turn, k3, pass the second and third sts over and off of the right needle.

Oh, I was missing you.

Me?

Mother Hen
BODY

Cast on 9 sts with Firefly, placing 3 sts on each of three dpns. Join to work in the round, being careful not to twist the stitches. Place a stitch marker on the first stitch.

Rnd 1: Knit.

Rnd 2: Kfb in each st—6 sts per needle, 18 sts total.

Rnd 3: Knit.

Rnd 4: Kfb in each st—12 sts per needle, 36 sts total.

Rnds 5 and 6: Knit.

Rnd 7: (k3, kfb); repeat to the end of the round—15 sts per needle, 45 sts total.

Rnd 8: Knit.

Rnd 9: (k4, kfb); repeat to the end of the round—18 sts per needle, 54 sts total.

Rnds 10 and 11: Knit.

Rnd 12: (k5, kfb); repeat to the end of the round—21 sts per needle, 63 sts total.

Place a stitch marker on round 12 and leave it there. Knit until the body measures 3 inches above the stitch marker.

Next rnd: Purl 1 round.

Continue on to make the outside body of the Mother Hen.

Switch to Ice Cream.

Knit 1 round.

Purl 1 round.

Knit every round until the body measures 3 inches above the purl round in Ice Cream.

Decrease Rounds

Rnd 1: (k5, k2tog); repeat to the end of the round—18 sts per needle, 54 sts rem.

Rnd 2: (k4, k2tog); repeat to the end of the round—15 sts per needle, 45 sts rem.

Rnds 3 and 4: Knit.

Rnd 5: (k3, k2tog); repeat to the end of the round—12 sts per needle, 36 sts rem.

Rnd 6: Knit.

Rnd 7: (k2, k2tog); repeat to the end of the round—9 sts per needle, 27 sts rem.

Rnds 8 and 9: Knit.

Rnd 10: (k1, k2tog); repeat to the end of the round—6 sts per needle, 18 sts rem.

Rnd 11: Knit.

Rnd 12: K2tog; repeat to the end of the round—3 sts per needle, 9 sts rem.

Cut the yarn, thread it on a yarn needle, and draw it through the remaining sts, pulling tight to close the hole. Take a few stitches to secure. Push the Firefly half of the body up into the Ice Cream half and take a few more stitches to secure the halves together. Pull the end in between the layers and trim.

NECK AND HEAD

Neck

Cast on 24 sts with Ice Cream, placing 8 sts on each of three dpns. Join to work in the round, being careful not to twist the stitches. Place a stitch marker on the first stitch.

Rnds 1–3: Knit.

Rnd 4: (ssk, k4, k2tog); repeat on each needle—6 sts per needle, 18 sts rem.

Rnds 5–8: Knit.

Rnd 9: (k1, m1, knit 5 sts); repeat to the end of the round—7 sts per needle, 21 sts total.

Rnds 10–14: Knit.

Head

Rnd 15: (k5, k2tog); repeat on each needle—6 sts per needle, 18 sts rem.

Rnd 16: (k4, k2tog); repeat on each needle—5 sts per needle, 15 sts rem.

Rnd 17: Knit.

Rnd 18: (k3, k2tog); repeat on each needle—4 sts per needle, 12 sts rem.

Rnd 19: (k2, k2tog); repeat on each needle—3 sts per needle, 9 sts rem.

Cut the yarn, thread it on a yarn needle, and draw it through the remaining sts, pulling tight to close the

hole. Stitch to secure. Stuff the neck and head lightly with fiberfill. Thread the cast-on end on a yarn needle and whipstitch the neck to the body.

WING / TAIL (Make 3)

Cast on 9 sts with Ice Cream, placing 3 sts on each of three dpns. Join to work in the round, being careful not to twist the stitches. Place a stitch marker on the first stitch.

Rnd 1: Knit.

Rnd 2: (k1, m1, k1, m1, k1); repeat on each needle—15 sts.

Rnd 3: Knit.

Rnd 4: K7, mb, k7.

Rnd 5: Knit.

Repeat rounds 4 and 5 until the wing/tail measures 1½ inches from the cast-on edge, ending with a round 4.

Decrease Rounds

Rnd 1: On Needle 1, k3, k2tog—4 sts rem. On Needle 2, ssk, k1, k2tog—3 sts rem. On Needle 3, k2tog, k3—4 sts rem; 11 sts total rem.

Yes, you! Now get under here with the rest of the eggs. Make room, everyone!

Rnd 2: On Needles 1 and 3, knit. On Needle 2, k1, mb, k1.

Rnd 3: On Needles 1 and 3, k2tog twice—2 sts per needle rem. On Needle 2, knit—7 sts rem.

Rnd 4: On Needles 1 and 3, knit. On Needle 2, k1, mb, k1.

Rnd 5: Knit.

Cut the yarn, thread it on a yarn needle, and draw it through the remaining sts, pulling tight. Lay the piece flat so the bobbles make an edge. Pull the end to the inside of the wing/tail and trim.

Thread the tail from the cast-on sts on a yarn needle and take some stitches to close the hole. Then whipstitch the wing to the side of the body, stitching upward along the end and continuing across the top of the wing for about four stitches to secure. Whipstitch the tail so it stands up straight. Pull all ends to the inside and trim.

CROWN

Cast on 5 sts with Firecracker. Use two dpns to knit back and forth.

Row 1: Knit.

Row 2: Mb, k1, mb, k1, mb.

Row 3: Knit.

Bind off. Cut the yarn and draw it through the remaining st. Whipstitch the cast-on and bound-off edges together. Whipstitch the crown to the top of the head. Pull the end to the inside of the crown and trim to stay inside.

BEAK

Cast on 3 sts with Pollen. Use two dpns to knit back and forth.

Row 1: Mb, k1, mb.

Bind off. Cut the yarn and draw it through the remaining st. Whipstitch the cast-on and bound-off edges together. Form the two bobbles into a beak shape. Whipstitch the beak to the front of the head, lining it up with the crown. Pull the end to the inside and trim.

EYES

With a length of black embroidery floss threaded on an embroidery needle, take 2 small straight stitches to form a V for each eye, using the photo on page 56 as a guide.

Chicks (Make 4)
BODY

Cast on 9 sts with Firefly, placing 3 sts on each of three dpns. Join to work in the round, being careful not to twist the stitches. Place a stitch marker on the first stitch.

Rnd 1: Knit.

Rnd 2: (k2, kfb); repeat to the end of the round—4 sts per needle, 12 sts total.

Rnd 3: Knit.

Rnd 4: (k3, kfb); repeat to the end of the round—5 sts per needle, 15 sts total.

Place a stitch marker on round 4 and leave it there. Knit every round until the chick measures 1 inch above the stitch marker.

Decrease Rounds

Rnd 1: (k3, k2tog); repeat to the end of the round—4 sts per needle, 12 sts rem.

Rnd 2: (k2, k2tog); repeat to the end of the round—3 sts per needle, 9 sts rem.

At this point, thread the tail from the cast-on sts on a yarn needle. Take some stitches to close the hole. Pull the end to the inside and trim.

Fill the chick about halfway full with plastic pellets and the rest with fiberfill or stuff only with fiberfill until firm. Continue to stuff to the end.

Rnd 3: Knit.

BEAK

Switch to Pollen.

Rnd 1: Knit.

Rnd 2: (k1, k2tog); repeat to the end of the round—2 sts per needle, 6 sts rem.

Rnd 3: K2tog; repeat to the end of the round—1 st per needle, 3 sts rem.

Finish any stuffing. Cut the yarn, thread it on a yarn needle, and draw it through the remaining sts, pulling tight to close the hole. Stitch to secure, pull the end to the inside of the body, and trim.

What? You think I'm an *egg*?

Well, Spud, you *are* round and white.

WINGS (Make 2 per Chick)

With Firefly and two dpns, pick up 3 sts about ½ inch down from the beak. Working back and forth, knit 2 rows.

Next row: K1, k2tog, pass the first st over the second st and off the needle. Cut the yarn and draw the tail through the remaining st. Weave the ends in and trim.

Place the second wing directly across from the first wing on the opposite side of the chick.

EYES

With a length of black embroidery floss threaded on an embroidery needle, make two French knots for the eyes.

Eggshells (Make 4)

Cast on 18 sts with Ice Cream, placing 6 sts on each of three dpns. Join to work in the round, being careful not to twist the stitches. Place a stitch marker on the first stitch.

Knit every round until the eggshell measures 1 inch from the cast-on edge.

Decrease Rounds

Rnd 1: (k4, k2tog); repeat on each needle—5 sts per needle, 15 sts rem.

Rnd 2: (k3, k2tog); repeat on each needle—4 sts per needle, 12 sts rem.

Rnd 3: Knit.

Rnd 4: (k2, k2tog); repeat on each needle—3 sts per needle, 9 sts rem.

Cut the yarn, thread it on a yarn needle, and draw it through the remaining sts, pulling tight to close the hole. Stitch to secure and pull the end to the inside of the egg. Weave in ends and trim.

Wrong story. . . .
I guess the
yolk's on me.

Are you my
mother?

Barn Cat

Barn Cat is a sly fellow always perched and ready to pounce . . . into the nearest spot for a nap. With sweetly colored stripes and soft white paws, Barn Cat works up quickly and keeps the knitting interesting at the same time.

Finished Measurements
6 inches tall, 3 inches wide, 2½ inches long from the front to the back of the body

Yarn
Spud & Chloë Sweater (55% superwash wool, 45% organic cotton; 100 grams/160 yards), 1 hank each in Pollen #7508, Firefly #7505, Ice Cream #7500, and Watermelon #7512

Needles
U.S. size 6 (4 mm) double-pointed needles (set of four) or size needed to obtain gauge

Notions
Stitch markers
Ruler or tape measure
Yarn needle
Scissors
Plastic pellets (optional—do not use for young children or babies, as they pose a choking hazard)
Polyester fiberfill
Embroidery needle
Black embroidery floss

Gauge
5½ sts per inch in stockinette stitch

Excuse me, Mr. Barn Cat. Maybe we should keep going . . .

I need to be around a barn cat like I need to be around a sheep shearing.

BODY

Starting at the bottom of the body with Firefly, cast on 9 sts, placing 3 sts on each of three dpns. Join to work in the round, being careful not to twist the stitches. Place a stitch marker on the first stitch.

Rnd 1: Knit.

Rnd 2: Kfb in each st—6 sts per needle, 18 sts total.

Rnd 3: Knit.

Rnd 4: Kfb in each st—12 sts per needle, 36 sts total.

Rnd 5: Knit.

Rnd 6: (k2, kfb); repeat to the end of the round—16 sts per needle, 48 sts total. Place a stitch marker on round 6 and leave it there.

Switch to Pollen and begin the stripe pattern. **Note:** While working the stripes, carry the yarns along the inside of the body.

Rnds 7 and 8: Knit.

Switch to Firefly.

Rnds 9 and 10: Knit.

Repeat rounds 7–10 until the body measures 2½ inches above the stitch marker left on round 6.

Decrease Rounds

Continue in the stripe pattern, alternating colors every 2 rounds.

Rnd 1: (k2, k2tog); repeat to the end of the round—12 sts per needle, 36 sts rem.

Rnd 2: Knit.

Rnd 3: (k1, k2tog); repeat to the end of the round—8 sts per needle, 24 sts rem.

At this point, thread the end from the cast-on sts at the bottom of the body on a yarn needle and take a few stitches to close the hole. Pull the end to the inside of the body and trim. Fill the body one-third full with plastic pellets and stuff the rest with fiberfill *or* stuff with fiberfill only. Continue to add stuffing as needed.

Rnd 4: Knit.

Rnd 5: K2tog; repeat to the end of the round—4 sts per needle, 12 sts rem.

Rnd 6: (k1, k2tog, k1); repeat to the end of the round—3 sts per needle, 9 sts rem.

Finish any stuffing. Cut the yarn, thread it on a yarn needle, and draw it through the remaining sts, pulling tight to close the hole. Take a few stitches to secure. Leave the end out to use later for attaching the head.

HEAD

Starting at the back of the head with Firefly, cast on 9 sts, placing 3 sts on each of three dpns. Join to work in the round, being careful not to twist the stitches. Place a stitch marker on the first stitch.

Rnd 1: Knit.

Place a stitch marker on round 9 and leave it there. Continue to knit every round, alternating colors every 2 rounds, until the head measures 1½ inches above the stitch marker.

Decrease Rounds

Continue in Firefly only.

Rnd 1: (k5, k2tog); repeat to the end of the round—12 sts per needle, 36 sts rem.

Rnd 2: (k4, k2tog); repeat to the end of the round—10 sts per needle, 30 sts rem.

Rnds 3 and 4: Knit.

At this point, thread the end from the cast-on sts at the back of the head on a yarn needle and take a few stitches to close the hole. Pull the end to the inside and trim. Stuff the head with fiberfill and continue to stuff to the end.

Rnd 5: (k3, k2tog); repeat to the end of the round—8 sts per needle, 24 sts rem.

Switch to Ice Cream.

Rnd 2: Kfb in each st—6 sts per needle, 18 sts total.

Switch to Pollen.

Rnd 3: Knit.

Rnd 4: Kfb in each st—12 sts per needle, 36 sts total.

Switch to Firefly and continue to alternate Firefly and Pollen every 2 rounds.

Rnds 5–8: Knit.

Rnd 9: (k5, kfb); repeat to the end of the round—14 sts per needle, 42 sts total.

Huh, can't you see that I'm *busy*!?

Weren't you just sleeping?

Rnds 6–9: Knit.

Rnd 10: (k2, k2tog); repeat to the end of the round—6 sts per needle, 18 sts rem.

Rnd 11: Knit.

Rnd 12: (k1, k2tog); repeat to the end of the round—4 sts per needle, 12 sts rem.

Rnd 13: (k1, k2tog, k1); repeat to the end of the round—3 sts per needle, 9 sts rem.

Finish any stuffing. Cut the yarn, thread it on a yarn needle, and draw it through the remaining sts, pulling tight to close the hole. Stitch to secure, pull the end to the inside of the head, and trim.

Thread the end from the top of the body on a yarn needle and whipstitch the head to the body.

EARS (Make 2)

Outer Ear

Cast on 7 sts with Firefly. Use two dpns to work back and forth.

Row 1: Knit.

Row 2: Purl.

Rows 3 and 4: Repeat rows 1 and 2.

Row 5: K1, ssk, k1, k2tog, k1—5 sts rem.

Row 6: Purl.

Row 7: Ssk, k1, k2tog—3 sts rem.

Row 8: P3tog—1 st rem.

Cut the yarn and pull the end through the remaining st.

Inner Ear

Cast on 5 sts with Watermelon. Use two dpns to work back and forth.

Row 1: Knit.

Row 2: Purl.

Rows 3 and 4: Repeat rows 1 and 2.

Row 5: Ssk, k1, k2tog—3 sts rem.

Row 6: P3tog—1 st rem.

Cut the yarn, leaving an 8-inch end. Pull the end through the remaining st.

Hold the inner ear and outer ear together with the purl sides facing each other. Thread an end from the inner ear on a yarn needle and whipstitch the inner ear to the outer ear. Thread the end from the cast-on sts of the outer ear on a yarn needle and whipstitch the ear to the top of the head. Pull all ends to the inside of the head and trim.

FACE

Nose

With a length of Watermelon threaded on a yarn needle, use straight stitches to make a nose, using the photo on page 64 as a guide.

Mouth

With a length of black embroidery floss threaded on an embroidery needle, take 3 straight stitches to form the mouth and the centerline down from the nose. Pull all ends to the inside of the head and trim.

Eyes

Thread a length of black embroidery floss on an embroidery needle, take 2 small horizontal straight stitches for each eye. Then take a tiny vertical straight stitch to pull the horizontal straight stitches slightly upward.

Whiskers

Thread a length of black embroidery floss on an embroidery needle. Stitching through the nose from one side to the other, draw the floss through halfway so equal amounts hang on either side of the nose. Take the floss off of the needle and repeat the process with another length of floss, right next to the first. Tie the two threads on each side together with a half-knot to secure the whiskers. Trim to desired length.

TAIL

Cast on 9 sts with Firefly, placing 3 sts on each of three dpns. Join to work in the round, being careful not to twist the stitches. Place a stitch marker on the first stitch.

Rnds 1 and 2: Knit.

Switch to Pollen.

Rnds 3 and 4: Knit.

Rnds 5–12: Repeat rounds 1–4.

Switch to Firefly.

Rnd 13: Knit.

Rnd 14: (k1, m1, k1, m1, k1); repeat on each needle—5 sts per needle, 15 sts total.

Rnd 15: Knit.

Switch to Ice Cream.

Rnds 16–18: Knit.

Rnd 19: (ssk, k1, k2tog); repeat on each needle—3 sts per needle, 9 sts rem.

Rnd 20: Knit.

Rnd 21: (k1, k2tog, pass the first st over the second st and off the right

No, I'm busy looking for mice.

Okay, we'll be on our way. Don't mind us.

needle); repeat on each needle—1 st per needle, 3 sts rem.

Cut the yarn, thread it on a yarn needle, and draw it through the remaining sts, pulling tight to close the hole. Pull the end to the inside of the tail and trim. Stuff the tail lightly with fiberfill.

Thread the end from the cast-on sts on a yarn needle. Whipstitch the tail to the bottom and center of the back of the body. Pull the end to the inside of the body and trim.

BACK PAWS (Make 2)

Cast on 12 sts with Ice Cream, placing 4 sts on each of three dpns. Join to work in the round, being careful not to twist the stitches. Place a stitch marker on the first stitch.

Rnds 1–4: Knit.

Rnd 5: (k1, m1, k2, m1, k1); repeat on each needle—6 sts per needle, 18 sts total.

Rnds 6 and 7: Knit.

Rnd 8: (ssk, k2, k2tog); repeat on each needle—4 sts per needle, 12 sts total.

Place the first 6 sts on the first needle. Place the last 6 sts on a second needle. Cut the yarn and thread it on a yarn needle. Use the Kitchener stitch to close the end of the paw. Pull the end to the inside of

the paw and trim. Stuff the paw lightly with fiberfill.

Thread the end from the cast-on sts on a yarn needle and whipstitch the cast-on end of the paw closed. Whipstitch the paw to the bottom and slightly to the side of the body, using the photo as a guide. Pull the end to the inside of the body and trim.

FRONT PAWS (Make 2)

Cast on 10 sts with Ice Cream, placing 3 sts on Needles 1 and 2 and 4 sts on

Needle 3. Join to work in the round, being careful not to twist the stitches. Place a stitch marker on the first stitch.

Rnds 1 and 2: Knit.

Rnd 3: On Needles 1 and 2, (k1, m1, k2) on each needle—4 sts per needle. On Needle 3, k1, m1, k2, m1, k1—6 sts; 14 sts total.

Rnds 4 and 5: Knit.

Rnd 6: (ssk, k3, k2tog); repeat to the end of the round—10 sts rem.

Place the first 5 sts on the first needle. Place the last 5 sts on a second needle. Cut the yarn and thread it on a yarn needle. Use the Kitchener stitch to close the end of the paw. Pull the end to the inside of the paw and trim. Stuff the paw lightly with fiberfill.

Thread the tail end from the cast-on sts on a yarn needle. Whipstitch the cast-on end of the paw closed. Whipstitch the paw to the bottom front of the body, using the photo on page 64 as a guide. Pull the end to the inside of the body and trim.

With a length of black embroidery floss threaded on an embroidery needle, take 2 straight stitches at the front of each paw, again using the photo as a guide. Pull all the ends to the inside of the paw and trim.

See you later, alligator.

In a while, huge white sheep.

Mice

Of course Barn Cat needs some mice around to keep him occupied. These mice can stand at attention or lie flat to the ground when they need to hide. You can get several mice out of one skein of yarn. This is also the perfect project to use up leftovers from the other projects or from your stash yarn.

Finished Measurements
3 inches long, not including the tail

Yarn
Spud & Chloë Sweater (55% superwash wool, 45% organic cotton; 100 grams/160 yards), 1 hank each in Ice Cream #7500 and Watermelon #7512

Needles
U.S. size 6 (4 mm) double-pointed needles (set of four) or size needed to obtain gauge

Notions
Stitch markers
Ruler or tape measure
Yarn needle
Scissors
Plastic pellets (optional—do not use for young children or babies, as they pose a choking hazard)
Polyester fiberfill
Embroidery needle
Black embroidery floss

Gauge
5½ sts per inch in stockinette stitch

Yeah, right under *there.*

We're kind of new here. Did you see where the big striped cat went?

BODY

Starting at the back end with Ice Cream, cast on 9 sts, placing 3 sts on each of three dpns. Join to work in the round, being careful not to twist the stitches. Place a stitch marker on the first stitch.

Rnd 1: Knit.

Rnd 2: Kfb in each st—6 sts per needle, 18 sts total.

Rnd 3: Knit.

Rnd 4: (k2, kfb); repeat to the end of the round—8 sts per needle, 24 sts total.

Place a stitch marker on round 4 and leave it there. Knit every round until the mouse measures 1¼ inches above the stitch marker.

Decrease Rounds

Rnd 1: Ssk, knit to the last 2 sts, k2tog—7 sts on Needles 1 and 3, 8 sts on Needle 2; 22 sts rem.

Rnd 2: Knit.

Rnds 3–6: Repeat rnds 1 and 2—5 sts on Needles 1 and 3, 8 sts on Needle 2; 18 sts rem.

Head

Note: The Needle 2 stitches are the underside of the mouse.

Rnd 1: On Needles 1 and 3, knit. On Needle 2, ssk, knit to the last 2 sts, k2tog—6 sts on Needle 2, 16 sts rem.

Rnd 2: On Needles 1 and 3, knit. On Needle 2, k2, k2tog, k2—5 sts per needle, 15 sts rem.

At this point, thread the end from the cast-on sts on a yarn needle and take several stitches to close the hole. Pull the end to the inside and trim. Fill the bottom with a layer of plastic pellets *or* stuff with fiberfill only. Continue to stuff the body as you finish the mouse.

Rnd 3: (k3, k2tog); repeat on each needle—4 sts per needle, 12 sts rem.

Rnd 4: Knit.

Rnd 5: (k2, k2tog); repeat on each needle—3 sts per needle, 9 sts rem.

Rnd 6: (k1, k2tog); repeat on each needle—2 sts per needle, 6 sts rem.

Finish any stuffing. Cut the yarn, thread it on a yarn needle, and draw it through the remaining sts, pulling tight to close the hole. Stitch to secure, pull the end to the inside of the body, and trim.

EARS (Make 2)

Cast on 6 sts with Watermelon, placing 2 sts on each of three dpns. Join to work in the round, being careful not to twist the stitches. Place a stitch marker on the first stitch.
Rnd 1: Knit.
Rnd 2: (k1, m1, k1) on each needle—3 sts per needle, 9 sts total.
Rnd 3: Knit.

Cut the yarn, thread it on a yarn needle, and draw it through the remaining sts, pulling tight to close the hole. Stitch to secure, pull the end to the inside of the ear, and trim. Flatten the ear. Thread the end from the cast-on sts on a yarn needle and whipstitch the ear to the top of the mouse, using the photo as a guide. Pull the ends to the inside of the head and trim.

TAIL

Cast on 2 sts with Watermelon. Use two dpns to work in I-cord until the tail measures 5 inches from the cast-on sts.
Next row: K2tog—1 st rem.

Cut the yarn, thread it on a yarn needle, and draw it through the remaining st. Weave the end to the inside of the tail. Trim the end close to the cord and pull inside. Thread the end from the cast-on sts on a yarn needle and whipstitch the tail to the back end of the mouse, stitching it on directly over the ring of cast-on sts. Pull the end to the inside of the body and trim.

FEET (Make 2)

Cast on 1 st loosely with Watermelon. Use two dpns to work back and forth.
Row 1: Knit in the front and back and front again—3 sts.
Row 2: Purl.
Row 3: Knit, do not turn, pass the second and third sts over the first st and off the needle—1 st rem.

Hee-hee! Made you say *underwear.*

Spud, that's not nice.

Under where?

Cut the yarn, thread it on a yarn needle, and draw it through the remaining st. Take some stitches to gather the foot into a ball shape and then whipstitch the foot to the lower front of the mouse, using the photo as a guide.

FACE

Note: Pull all ends to the inside of the head and trim.

Nose
With a length of Watermelon threaded on a yarn needle, take several straight stitches at the tip of the nose.

Eyes
With a length of black embroidery floss threaded on an embroidery needle, make a French knot for each eye.

Whiskers
Thread a length of black embroidery floss on an embroidery needle and stitch it through the nose, drawing the floss through halfway. Cut the yarn, and repeat to make a second whisker. Make a half-knot in each whisker on both sides of the nose to secure if necessary.

Tee-hee.
Can't help myself.

Let's keep looking for
Little Lamb.

Little Lamb

Little Lamb is the host with the most on Spud and Chloë's farm adventure. This project uses the same twisted loop stitch that's used on Spud, but on a smaller scale and in a dark brown. The result is a unique sheep with his own personality.

Finished Measurements
5½ inches tall, 3 inches wide,
3½ inches long from the front to
the back of the body

Yarn
Spud & Chloë Sweater (55% superwash wool, 45% organic cotton; 100 grams/160 yards), 1 hank each in Root Beer #7503 and Ice Cream #7500

Needles
U.S. size 6 (4 mm) double-pointed needles (set of four) or size needed to obtain gauge

Notions
Stitch markers
Ruler or tape measure
Yarn needle

Scissors
Polyester fiberfill
Embroidery needle
Black embroidery floss

Gauge
5½ sts per inch in stockinette stitch

Twisted Loop (tl)
Knit the st and leave it on the left needle, pull the loop out about 2 inches with your fingers, twist the loop until it twists back on itself, place the loop back on the left needle, knit 2 sts together.

Little Lamb!

It's Spud and Chloë, just in time for my grass-tasting party!

BODY

Starting at the bottom of the body with Root Beer, cast on 9 sts, placing 3 sts on each of three dpns. Join to work in the round, being careful not to twist the stitches. Place a stitch marker on the first stitch.

Rnd 1: Knit.

Rnd 2: Kfb in each st—6 sts per needle, 18 sts total.

Rnd 3: Knit.

Rnd 4: Kfb in each st—12 sts per needle, 36 sts total.

Rnd 5: Knit.

Rnd 6: (k2, kfb); repeat to the end of the round—16 sts per needle, 48 sts total. Place a stitch marker on round 6 and leave it there.

Begin pattern as follows:

Rnd 1: (tl, k1); repeat to the end of the round.

Rnd 2: Knit.

Rnd 3: (k1, tl); repeat to the end of the round.

Rnd 4: Knit.

Repeat rounds 1–4 until the body measures 2½ inches above the stitch marker, ending with a round 1.

Decrease Rounds

Rnd 1: (k2, k2tog); repeat to the end of the round—12 sts per needle, 36 sts rem.

Rnd 2: (k1, tl); repeat to the end of the round.

Rnd 3: (k1, k2tog); repeat to the end of the round—8 sts per needle, 24 sts rem.

At this point, thread the tail end from the cast-on sts on a yarn needle and take a few stitches to close the hole at the bottom of the body. Pull the end to the inside and trim. Stuff the body with fiberfill and continue to stuff as you work to the end of the body.

Rnd 4: (tl, k1); repeat to the end of the round.

Rnd 5: (k2tog); repeat to the end of the round—4 sts per needle, 12 sts rem.

Rnd 6: (k1, k2tog, k1); repeat to the end of the round—3 sts per needle, 9 sts rem.

Finish any stuffing. Cut the yarn, thread the tail on a yarn needle, and draw it through the remaining sts, pulling tight to close the hole. Take a few stitches to secure, pull the end to the inside of the body, and trim.

HEAD

Starting at the back of the head with Root Beer, cast on 9 sts, placing 3 sts on each of three dpns. Join to work in the round, being careful not to twist the stitches. Place a stitch marker on the first stitch.

Rnd 1: Knit.

Rnd 16: (ssk, k3, k2tog); repeat on each needle—5 sts per needle, 15 sts rem.

Rnd 17: Knit.

Rnd 18: (k3, k2tog); repeat on each needle—4 sts per needle, 12 sts rem.

After round 18, thread the tail end from the cast-on sts on a yarn needle and take some stitches to close the hole at the back of the head. Pull the end to the inside of the head and trim. Fill the head with fiberfill until firm. Continue adding stuffing until the Decrease rounds are completed.

Rnd 19: (k2, k2tog); repeat on each needle—3 sts per needle, 9 sts rem.

Add any final stuffing needed. Cut the yarn, thread it on a yarn needle, and draw it through the remaining sts, pulling tight to close the hole. Stitch to secure, pull the end to the inside of the head, and trim.

Rnd 2: (k1, m1, k1, m1, k1); repeat on each needle—5 sts per needle, 15 sts total.

Rnds 3 and 4: Knit.

Rnd 5: (k1 [k1, m1 four times]); repeat between (and) on each needle— 9 sts per needle, 27 sts total.

Rnds 6–11: Knit.

Switch to Ice Cream.

Rnd 12: Knit.

Rnd 13: (ssk, k5, k2tog); repeat on each needle—7 sts per needle, 21 sts rem.

Rnds 14 and 15: Knit.

Whoa! Now that's *my* kind of party.

With a length of Root Beer threaded on a yarn needle, whipstitch the head to the top front of the body. Pull the ends to the inside of the body and trim.

FEET (Make 4)
Cast on 12 sts with Ice Cream, placing 4 sts on each of three dpns. Join to work in the round, being careful not to twist the stitches. Place a stitch marker on the first stitch.
Rnds 1–6: Knit.
Rnd 7: (k2, k2tog) on each needle—3 sts per needle, 9 sts rem.
Rnd 8: Knit.
Cut the yarn, thread it on a yarn needle, and draw it through the remaining sts, pulling tight to close the hole. Stitch to secure, pull to the inside, and trim. Stuff the foot with fiberfill until firm. Thread the end from the cast-on sts on a yarn needle. Whipstitch the feet to the bottom of the body.

EARS (Make 2)
Cast on 6 sts with Root Beer, placing 2 sts on each of three dpns. Join to work in the round, being careful not to twist the stitches. Place a stitch marker on the first stitch.
Rnds 1 and 2: Knit.
Rnd 3: (k1, m1, k1); repeat on each

needle—3 sts per needle, 9 sts total.
Rnds 4 and 5: Knit.
Rnd 6: (k1, k2tog); repeat on each needle—2 sts per needle, 6 sts rem.
Cut the yarn, thread it on a yarn needle, and draw it through the remaining sts, pulling tight to close the hole. Stitch to secure, pull the end to the inside, and trim. Flatten out the ear. Thread the tail from the cast-on sts on a yarn needle and whipstitch the ears to the head, using the photograph as a guide. Pull the end to the inside of the head and trim.

TAIL

Cast on 9 sts with Root Beer, placing 3 sts on each of three dpns. Join to work in the round, being careful not to twist the stitches. Place a stitch marker on the first stitch.

Rnds 1–3: Knit.

Rnd 4: (k1, k2tog); repeat on each needle—2 sts per needle, 6 sts rem.

Cut the yarn, thread it on a yarn needle, and draw it through the remaining sts, pulling tight to close the hole. Stitch to secure, pull to the inside, and trim. Flatten out the tail. Thread the end from the cast-on sts on a yarn needle and whipstitch the tail to the back end, toward the top of the body. Pull the end to the inside of the body and trim.

HAIR

Cast on 4 sts with Root Beer. Use two dpns to work back and forth.

Row 1: TI in each st.

Row 2: Knit.

Rows 3 and 4: Repeat rows 1 and 2.

Row 5: Repeat row 1.

Bind off. Cut the yarn, thread it on a yarn needle, and draw it through the remaining st. Arrange and whipstitch the hair between the ears, on the top of the head. Pull the end through to the inside of the head and trim.

FACE

With an embroidery needle and a length of black embroidery floss, take 2 straight stitches to make each eye. Make a V using 2 straight stitches, then add 1 straight stitch coming down from the point of the V. Use the photo on page 78 as a guide. Pull all ends to the inside of the head and trim.

Farm Accessories

Just like in fashion, accessorizing is key on the farm! This section is filled with fun farm accessories to make playing with the knitted animals even better! There is a big red barn that is open for business, a white picket fence that can be formed into a pen or left open, colorful buckets for toting grass, chicks, or even a mouse, and a whole bunch of hay bales, because every farm has to feed its animals. These projects are fun to make and will complete your knitted farm with style.

Barn

Every farm needs a big red barn! This project is extra-versatile. The open construction makes it easy for the characters to come in and out through the big barn door. Kids can have imaginative play going on inside or outside the barn, or both at the same time with no fuss at all. The collapsible sides mean that the barn can lie flat, making storage a snap. Made on bigger needles, this project will come together in no time at all.

Finished Measurements
Front: 12 inches tall, 12 inches wide
Folding side panels: 7 inches tall,
6 inches wide

Yarn
Spud & Chloë Sweater (55% superwash wool, 45% organic cotton; 100 grams/160 yards), 2 hanks in Firecracker #7509 and a small amount of Ice Cream #7500 for embroidery

Needles
U.S. size 9 (5.5mm) or size needed to obtain gauge

Notions
Ruler or tape measure
Stitch holder
Scissors
Corrugated cardboard: two 12-inch squares, four 7 × 6-inch squares (**Note:** An old shipping box works well)
Pencil
Yarn needle

Gauge
4 sts per inch in stockinette stitch

FRONT OF BARN (Make 2)

Cast on 12 sts with Firecracker. Work in garter stitch (knit every row) until the piece measures 7 inches from the cast-on edge, ending with a wrong-side row. Cut the yarn and place the stitches on a stitch holder. Set aside.

Repeat, but do not cut the yarn.

Knit across the stitches on the needle: Using the backward loop method, cast on 24 sts. Place the 12 stitches from the stitch holder onto the needle and knit across; 48 sts total. Continue to work in garter stitch on these 48 stitches as follows:

Rows 1–7: Knit.
Row 8: K1, ssk, knit to the last 3 sts, k2tog, k1; 46 sts rem.
Row 9: Knit.

Repeat rows 8 and 9 nine times; 28 sts rem.

Continue to repeat only row 8 twelve times; 4 sts rem.
Next row: Ssk, k2tog; 2 sts rem.
Next row: K2tog; 1 st rem.

Cut the yarn and pull through the remaining stitch.

Place one of the knitted barn fronts on top of one of the cardboard squares and use it as a pattern to draw the barn shape on the cardboard, then cut the shape out. Repeat with the other square.

Sandwich the two cardboard shapes between the two knitted barn fronts. Thread a length of Firecracker on a yarn needle and whipstitch the two barn fronts together. Pull the ends to the inside and trim.

SIDES (Make 2)

Note: The side uses a double knitting technique, which works up both sides at once.

Cast on 48 sts with Firecracker.

Row 1: (k1, sl1); repeat to the end of the row.

Repeat row 1 until the side measures 7 inches from the cast-on edge.

Gently pull the needle out of all of the stitches. Separate the stitches to form a tube. Turn the tube inside out so the knit side is facing out. With both needle tips facing to the right, place the needles back into the stitches, with the 24 sts from one side of the tube on one needle and the other 24 sts on the second needle.

Cut the yarn, leaving an 8-inch length, and thread it on a yarn needle. Place two 7 × 6-inch cardboard pieces inside the tube. Use the Kitchener stitch to close the top. Pull the end to the inside and trim.

FINISHING

With a cut length of Ice Cream threaded on a yarn needle, use the backstitch to embroider a 2½ x 3-inch rectangle on the front center of the barn. Backstitch an X on the inside of the rectangle. Wrap the yarn over and under the backstitches (this is sometimes called "couching"). The wraps should be close together, covering the backstitches completely. Pull the ends to the inside and trim.

Lay the barn front on a table with the back side facing up. Lay the barn sides along the sides of the front. With a cut length of Firecracker threaded on a yarn needle, whipstitch the barn sides to the barn front, making sure the sides fold and meet in the middle without overlapping. Pull all ends to the inside and trim.

Hay Bales

Stack them up, knock them down, play hide-and-seek, or make your farm friends have a seat. The hay bales add an interactive element to your farm set. By making the bales up in a super bulky yarn, you'll have a stack to play with in a jiffy.

Finished Measurements
3 inches high, 4 inches long

Yarn
Spud & Chloë Outer (65% superwash wool, 35% organic cotton; 100 grams/60 yards), 2 hanks (makes 3 hay bales) in Cornsilk #7208

Needles
U.S. size 15 (10 mm) or size needed to obtain gauge

Notions
Scissors
Yarn needle
1 sheet of regular-density foam,
1 inch × 15 inches × 17 inches

Gauge
2 sts per inch in stockinette stitch

BALE

Cast on 10 sts.

Row 1: Knit.

Row 2: Purl.

Rows 3–8: Repeat rows 1 and 2.

Rows 9 and 10: Knit.

Row 11: K10, cast on 6 sts.

Row 12: P16, cast on 6 sts.

Row 13: Knit.

Row 14: Purl.

Rows 15–18: Repeat rows 13 and 14.

Row 19: Knit.

Row 20: P6, k10, p6.

Row 21: Bind off 6 sts, k to end.

Row 22: Bind off 6 sts, p to end.

Row 23: Knit.

Row 24: Purl.

Rows 25–28: Repeat rows 23 and 24.

Rows 29–31: Knit.

Row 32: Purl.

Rows 33–38: Repeat rows 31 and 32.

Row 39: Knit.

Bind off.

Cut the yarn and pull the end through the remaining st.

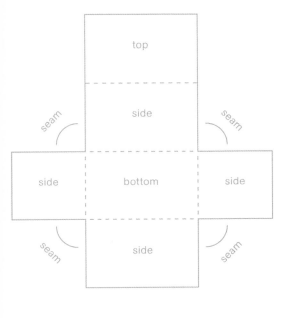

FINISHING

With a length of Cornsilk threaded on a yarn needle, whipstitch each of the four sides of the hay bale. This creates a box with an open lid.

Cut a 3-×-4-inch piece of foam. Place the foam piece in the bottom of the box. Fold the top of the hay bale over the foam. With a length of Cornsilk threaded on a yarn needle, whipstitch the top of the hay bale to the sides.

Weave all of the ends to the inside and trim.

- - - - - - - - - fold lines

Good-bye. See you soon!

That wasn't so bad.

Oh, we had a wonderful time. Thank you!

Picket Fence

When I designed this project, I found out that the horizontal boards on a picket fence are called "stringers." I love learning new facts like that! This fence is created with yarn, craft sticks, and a little fabric glue. The joins are flexible so you can make a corral or have an open fence.

Finished Measurements
6 inches high, 32 inches long

Yarn
Spud & Chloë Sweater (55% superwash wool, 45% organic cotton; 100 grams/160 yards), 1 hank in Ice Cream #7500

Needles
U.S. size 8 (5 mm) double-pointed needles (set of two) or size needed to obtain gauge

Notions
Ruler or tape measure
U.S. size F (4 mm) crochet hook
Yarn needle
Scissors
Craft sticks (6 inches × ¾ inch × ¹⁄₁₆ inch)
Fabric glue

Gauge
4½ sts per inch in stockinette stitch

POSTS (Make 10)

Cast on 8 sts. Using two dpns, work in I-cord for 6½ inches. Leave the stitches on the needle. There will be a gap running up the length of the I-cord where you are carrying the yarn across the back of the cord. There are bars or rungs going up the gap.

At the cast-on end of the I-cord, at the bottommost bar, use the crochet hook to twist a loop, with the bar around the hook. Put the crochet hook under the next bar and pull it through the loop on the crochet hook. Repeat this all the way up to the stitches on the needle. Transfer the loop on the crochet hook to a dpn— 9 sts.

Thread the end from the cast-on sts on a yarn needle. Take stitches to gather and close up the hole. Secure the end, pull to the inside of the post, and trim.

Place one craft stick inside the I-cord. Cut the yarn, thread it on a yarn needle, and draw it through the remaining sts, pulling tight to close the hole. Stitch to secure, then pull the end to the inside of the post and trim.

STRINGERS (Make 2)

Begin and work the same as for the post, but work until the stringer measures 32 inches from the cast-on edge. Finish the same as for the post.

Slide 5 craft sticks inside the I-cord, leaving a ½-inch gap between each stick. Finish by closing the end of the stringer the same as for the post.

FINISHING

Lay the posts out on a table. Place the stringers on top of the posts and arrange the posts so there are two posts on each stick in the stringers, as evenly spaced as possible. The bottom stringer should be placed 2 inches from the bottom of the posts. The top stringer should be placed 1 inch from the top of the posts, creating a 1-inch gap between the stringers.

Place a dime-size drop of fabric glue on the post where the stringer will be attached. Glue the stringers onto the posts. Let dry completely.

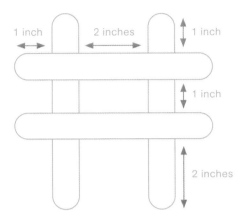

Did you have fun, Spud?

Oh, I *did*.

Buckets

Buckets are a necessity in farm life. You can carry water or food for the animals, and in this instance the mice or chicks fit in the buckets nicely. Use a variety of colors and leftovers to whip up some buckets to make your farm complete.

Finished Measurements
2 inches high without the handle,
2 inches wide

Yarn
Spud & Chloë Sweater (55% superwash wool, 45% organic cotton; 100 grams/160 yards), 1 hank each in Grass #7502, Popsicle #7501, and Moonlight #7507

Needles
U.S. size 6 (4 mm) double-pointed needles (set of four) or size needed to obtain gauge

Notions
Stitch markers
Ruler or tape measure
Scissors
Yarn needle

Gauge
5½ sts per inch in stockinette stitch

Me, too. Let's go back in a week or two for another visit.

BUCKET

Cast on 36 sts with the selected color, placing 12 sts on each of three dpns. Join to work in the round, being careful not to twist the stitches. Place a stitch marker on the first stitch.

Rnd 1: Knit.

Rnd 2: Purl.

Knit every round until the bucket measures 1 inch from the cast-on edge.

Decrease Rounds

Rnd 1: (k10, k2tog); repeat on each needle—11 sts per needle, 33 sts rem.

Rnds 2 and 3: Knit.

Rnd 4: (k9, k2tog); repeat on each needle—10 sts per needle, 30 sts rem.

Rnds 5 and 6: Knit.

Rnd 7: Purl.

Rnd 8: Knit.

Rnd 9: (k3, k2tog); repeat to the end of the round—8 sts per needle, 24 sts rem.

Rnd 10: (k2, k2tog); repeat to the end of the round—6 sts per needle, 18 sts rem.

Rnd 11: Knit.

Rnd 12: (k1, k2tog); repeat to the end of the round—4 sts per needle, 12 sts rem.

Rnd 13: (k2tog); repeat to the end of the round—2 sts per needle, 6 sts rem.

Cut the yarn, thread it on a yarn needle, and draw it through the remaining sts, pulling tight to close the hole. Pull the end to the inside of the bucket, weave in, and trim.

HANDLE

Cast on 2 sts. Using two dpns, work in I-cord until the handle measures 6 inches. Bind off. Cut the yarn, thread it on a yarn needle, and draw it through the remaining st. Make a small loop at the end of the cord and stitch to secure. Repeat at the cast-on end of the handle. Whipstitch the loops to the sides of the bucket. Weave in all ends and trim.

Well, maybe in a year or two.

Oh, Spud.

Acknowledgments

Spud & Chloë at the Farm is the product of countless hours put in by many contributors, not just me alone. There are many people I must thank.

Back in 2004, I mailed a small box stuffed with a few patterns and a knitted baby hat to Artisan Books. This started me on an amazingly fortunate path, since Ann Bramson, Artisan's publisher, embraced that initial proposal. Without Ann's faith and constant support, I could not have produced four beautiful knitting books so far.

My editor at Artisan, Trent Duffy, provides constant guidance and support. Beyond his knowledge of all things book-related, his sense of humor keeps me going through the sometimes arduous process of bookmaking.

Suzanne Lander, my production editor, has been an inspiring addition to the Artisan team. Her background in juvenile publishing was incredibly helpful as we brainstormed ideas for the Spud & Chloë storyline that appears in this book. (Not to mention how much I still appreciate her flagging down a taxi for me the last time I was visiting New York during a nor'easter—that's what I call support!) Suzanne also arranged for the invaluable assistance of Keonaona Peterson, who is a fantastic copy editor—her knowledge of knitting has proven invaluable to me.

Also at Artisan, I'd like to thank Erin Sainz, Bridget Heiking, Nancy Murray, Barbara Peragine, and Ian Gross. Art director Jan Derevjanik, who's worked on all my books, found the talented Amy Cartwright to do the line drawings in this one, and Susan Baldaserini provided a fabulous design. Amy Corley has been an energetic and enthusiastic publicist.

Photographer Liz Banfield has also been a part of my team from the start. I am so fortunate to reap the benefits of her vision here again. Her assistants, Ashley Miller and Sarah Jane Walter, also deserve much gratitude—and a special thanks to Lisa from Artsy Digs in Minneapolis. A big thanks also goes to Jim Mueller for my author photo.

Recently, I have a new family—at Spud & Chloë. First and foremost, I thank Linda Niemeyer for giving me this opportunity. Linda's creativity inspires me continually, and I appreciate her support, trust, and love. The rest of the team at Spud & Chloë/Blue Sky Alpacas is absolutely the best; thanks go to Merri Fromm, Valerie Teppo, Karen Rolstad, Nate Hager, and Colleen Powley. I do need to single out Merri, who helped with the pattern editing and found and organized a platoon of test knitters, all of whom also deserve praise: Martha Alvarado, Jess Bandelin, Christina Hammond, Ellen Huber, Catherine Mueller, Susan Seltz, Valerie Teppo, Sarah Walker, Heather Woods, and Merri herself.

I would like to give my family a big, huge hug for their ongoing love and support. My four kids and my husband have made the last twenty-one years more fun than anyone deserves.

Finally, I want to acknowledge my readers—the knitters who buy and use my books. You always surprise me with your energy and your willingness to take chances and to share your comments, e-mails, and loyalty. I have learned so much from all of you.

Good-bye. See you soon!

That wasn't so bad.

Oh, we had a
wonderful time.
Thank you!

The End